AF615112

CELESTIAL SONG/GOBIND GEET

CELESTIAL SONG/GOBIND GEET

The Dynamic Dialogue Between Guru Gobind Singh and Banda Singh Bahadur

SWAMI RAMA

The Himalayan International Institute
of Yoga Science and Philosophy of the U.S.A.
Honesdale, Pennsylvania

© 1986 Swami Rama
Himalayan International Institute
of Yoga Science and Philosophy of the U.S.A.
RR 1, Box 400
Honesdale, Pennsylvania 18431

First Printing 1986

All rights reserved. No part of this book may be reproduced in any form or by any means without permission in writing from the publisher. Printed in the United States of America.

The paper used in this publication meets the minimum requirements of American National Standard for Information Sciences—Permanence of Paper for Printed Library Materials, ANSI Z39.48-1984. ♾

ISBN 0-89389-102-9 *(hardcover)*
ISBN 0-89389-103-7 *(paperback)*

Contents

Preface

I have been contemplating the philosophy of Sikhism for a long time, but my recent visit to Chandigarh, Punjab, inspired and prompted me to write this book—*Celestial Song/Gobind Geet.* It is the dialogue between Sri Guru Gobind Singh and Banda Singh Bahadur, two great leaders in the history of humanity. These two figures are not fictional but factual. By learning of their epic lives and profound encounter, readers will understand that there have lived such great men on the earth, whose lives have been unparalleled, matchless, and exemplary. There is no other example in the history of the East or West to compare to that of Guru Gobind Singh and Banda Bahadur. They will be forever remembered by the people of India for their dedication and sacrifice. Just as in the Bhagavad Gita, in which Krishna and Arjuna are two outstanding figures, so in Sikh history Guru Gobind Singh and Banda Bahadur are two unique and great personalities. My love and reverence for them are enormous, long-standing, and profound.

I was already in the process of putting Sri Guru Granth Sahib* into poetry when I began to write this book. Then, whatever time I could steal from my busy schedule I spent in rhyming the couplets for *Gobind Geet.* Poetic form has been used throughout its eighteen chapters so that children and students can remember the message more easily. The philosophy expressed in this book has been taken from Guru Granth Sahib, Japji*, and Dasam Granth*. The history and philosophy of Sikh *dharma**

*Asterisked terms are defined in the glossary.

is also briefly explained. Although the dialogue between Guru Gobind Singh and Banda Bahadur is purely imaginary, the event actually took place, and I found it an excellent medium for explaining Sikh dharma.

India has long been the stronghold of yogis and sages, such as Kabir, Tulsi Das, Sur Das, Tukaram, Sant Janeswar, Sri Ram Das, and many others, but Sri Guru Nanak Dev, the founder of Sikh dharma, was unique. His teachings, which spread far and wide, made a lasting impact, leading the people to a national mission. The guru* lineage established by Sri Guru Nanak Dev remained vibrant and unbroken for two hundred years. This is evidence of the greatness of Guru Nanak Dev and his teaching, because this did not happen in the case of other sages, whose successors were not able to emanate the same intensity of wisdom and divine light as the originator. This is the reason that I revere Sri Guru Nanak Dev. He has been a great source of wisdom to one and all—a true guru who shines light upon the path and leads the aspirant to the final goal.

Sri Guru Nanak Dev founded Sikh dharma to establish harmony between diverse traditions. He was a pioneer sage who equally revered the essentials of all traditions. He reformed the Hindu* dharma by taking away the non-essentials and embracing the *bhakti* pantha** (path of love) in a practical way. His followers became a unique and strong community called Sikhs, which means "selfless servers." The Sikh philosophy originally sprang from the source of the Vedas* and the sayings of the sages, as did also Buddhism* and Jainism*. Sikh dharma was revered and embraced by Hindu and Muslim* alike, uniting the people and awakening their social and spiritual awareness.

The sayings of Guru Nanak Dev were compiled by Sri Arjan Devji, the fifth of the ten Sikh gurus, in the Sri Guru Granth Sahib, or Adi Granth*—the First Book. Among all the bibles of the world, the Sikh bible is the easiest to contemplate upon, understand, and practice. It is written in a lucid and simple script called Gurmukhi, which means "emanating from the mouth of the perfect and divine." The Adi Granth, which contains the writings of five other Sikh gurus and many sages from other backgrounds, describes the Sikh dharma beautifully. Its teachings are entirely harmonious with those found in the Upanishads* and the Bhagavad Gita*.

Sikhism is dedicated to upholding dharma. Dharma means the law that holds and sustains all in One. Its purpose is to attain a state of unity with the supreme Consciousness by removing all differences and inequalities between people, societies, and nations. By following the intrinsic, eternal law of dharma, one realizes one's latent potential for expressing truth and love. The perennial law of dharma is universal. It is described by all the great sages and spiritual traditions of the world. Its practical guidelines help people in social and spiritual development, leading the individual and the whole to the highest goal.

Dharma is different from religion. Religion is based on dogma, doctrines, customs, rules, and rituals; it is an institution with distinctive characteristics. Dharma is more subtle and profound than religion—it is universal and eternal. It is not bound by cultural, temporal, or theoretical differences, for it is the essential cohesive factor that unites all people in their highest potentials for human development. Truth, compassion, forbearance, forgiveness, integrity, and love are the hallmarks of dharma. It is the source of humanity's finest principles, qualities, virtues, and values. It is the inner network that supports all individuals and draws them to the Divine. Awareness of dharma breaks down all barriers between people, for it reveals our innate unity—that all people are members of one family.

Sikh dharma is based on selfless service to humanity and upholding dharma, regardless of the individual sacrifice required. There are no rituals or dogma in Sikh dharma, which is universal and egalitarian. Devotion is expressed inwardly by repetition of the Holy Name and externally through service to others. Sikh dharma is profound and expansive. It does not impose rigidity upon its adherents, but guides them to accept all and exclude none. It embraces compassion and *ahimsa** (non-harming) while dynamically maintaining health of body, mind, and spirit. Selfless action in the world is a spiritual path that leads to freedom. Sikh dharma practices cooperation, understanding, and solidarity to create and maintain a model society based on the laws of dharma. Sikh dharma accepts people of all sects, castes, creeds, and backgrounds, uniting them within love for the eternal, divine law of dharma.

The founder of Sikh dharma, Sri Guru Nanak Dev, was a great sage in tune with universal Truth, and he was also a great reformer and leader. He taught the people of his time that renunciation is not the way of the many, but of the rare individual. He proclaimed that selfless action performed skillfully and lovingly is the only way to lead the masses. He gave the message of fearlessness and self-confidence, and he showed the middle path. The middle path is not renunciation but selfless action, not attachment but dedication. Sikhism is unlike monism* and Buddhism, in which renunciation seems to be predominantly professed. Like the Bhagavad Gita, the Guru Granth Sahib teaches *bhakti pantha* and the way of performing selfless action, discarding the rigidity of rituals.

Sikhism believes in one absolute Reality beyond time, space, and causation, which is the formless, nameless, limitless, attributeless, and infinite universal Truth. That Reality is called Omkar; Om is the mother sound of the universe. The gist of Guru Nanak Dev's teaching is the path of love, which includes all and excludes none. It does not touch the extremes of being engrossed in the world or renouncing the world, but teaches one how to live in the world while remaining unaffected.

In the sixteenth and seventeenth centuries, there appeared ten Sikh gurus in succession, and all were great and dynamic. Guru Nanak Dev was the first. He was a great sage who loved peace and service, and his followers emulated these great qualities. But as Sikhism became established and grew strong, the Mogul* rulers, who were suppressing the people, began persecuting them. Finally, the people and their leaders could no longer bear the violent oppression, and acted to protect themselves. The tenth guru, Guru Gobind Singh, who established the Khalsa* order, was an avatar who sacrificed his life, children, and all that he had for the sake of dharma. A defender of dharma, Sri Guru Gobind Singh fought many battles and became victorious. With the help of his beloved disciple Banda, peace was finally reestablished, and the people were able to resume their harmonious way of life. The sacrifice that has been made by the guru lineage of the house of Nanak Dev should never be forgotten by the people of India. The Sikhs have always remained champions in protecting national integrity by upholding dharma and giving their lives for it.

Today the Sikh community is healthier and wealthier than the other communities in India, where the vast majority of people are economically deprived and suffer from malnutrition and illiteracy. Amid such disparity, the poor are easily converted by foreign missionaries offering the modern amenities of life. In time this could create a serious imbalance in Indian society, as more and more people forsake their age-old culture and values. But if the Sikhs become creative and embrace the deprived, it will help their countrymen to live more fully and to find value and practical purpose in their heritage. Hindus should welcome such a gesture, for the values of Sikh dharma and Hindu dharma are one and the same. Instead of doing reformation work, however, by establishing educational centers, libraries, and hospitals, Sikh leaders are using their resources to build marble *gurudwaras** (temples). If this trend continues, archeologists excavating the Punjab a few thousand years from now will find nothing but marble, and the Sikh tradition will be taken as the Marble Age.

The Sikh community today lacks a dynamic leader who can bind together all the factions of Sikh society and lead the community toward a better future. Communalism and fanaticism have increased to a high peak in Indian society, generating hatred, violence, and discord. But no positive method for treating this malady seems to be in the vision of the leaders of Sikhism or of India. If Sikhs and Hindus were to practice their ideals of universality, unity, and selfless service to the community, they would propagate these ideals, and the present difficult situation would ease.

Sikhs today do not like to identify themselves with the other communities of India, and I do not blame them. In the Sikh society there is not as much economic, social, and religious disparity, with its consequent impoverishment of living, thinking, and behaving, as is found in other factions of Indian society. Hindus do not like to accept this fact, and perhaps they do not want to be aware of it. No one wants to identify with the poor, illiterate, and downtrodden who make up the majority of Hindus.

In this book, the ideals of Sikh dharma are described in a simple and lucid way so they can be enjoyed, understood, and applied by all who hear them. The book begins with a description of Guru Nanak Dev and an appeal to Guru Gobind Singh to send someone to assist those suffering in the drama of life. Then the story opens with the two central characters, Guru Gobind Singh and Banda Bahadur, in their separate worlds: the battlefield and the hermitage. Finally the two meet, and their dialogue begins as they discuss their ancient bond and future mission. But Banda is attached to his role as monk, and so Guru Gobind engages him in a dialogue to convince him to accept dharma by serving humanity actively in the world. The guru instructs the disciple in the ways of dharma and directs him to uphold it by practicing the middle path. Then dharma is defined. Next a debate about responsible action, futility, and ahimsa occurs between the pacifist-renunciate and the warrior-saint. Banda is at last convinced to act, but he doubts his ability to change the collective destiny of humanity. Guru Gobind assures him it is possible, citing the examples of Sri Rama and Guru Nanak Dev. The importance of fighting against *adharma** (unrighteousness), and not merely against some sect, nation, or faction, is explained. Then the dualistic and non-dualistic views of life are discussed. Psychic powers are described as obstacles to growth, and the highest path—the essence of all—is revealed. Then the guru lineage, the guru, and the method of initiation are explained. Then are described the Divine, the Goddess, and the Holy Name. Finally Banda is convinced to leave the hermitage and serve others selflessly and dynamically in the world. He surrenders himself completely to Guru Nanak's lineage and is initiated into the Khalsa.

The main idea of the book is that the spiritually aware have a responsibility to help those in the world—that selfless service to humanity is, in fact, a spiritual practice. To serve, to remember, and to love are the three essential aspects of Sikh dharma. If all people will strive to apply these principles in their daily lives, then the flower of humanity will blossom. I hope readers will find this book beneficial, illuminating, and enlightening.

In India, that sacred land so beautiful and old,
There is a holy dialogue that's often been retold
Between Sri Guru Gobind Singh, designer so divine,
And his Banda Bahadur, defender so sublime.
This is their tale of destiny told now in verse and rhyme
So it may reinspire those of every place and time
To live in Truth and realize our unity above
By acting with these principles: remember, serve, and love.

Acknowledgments

It is a joy for me to acknowledge that Dr. Arpita worked with me throughout this book in rhyming and checking the meter. Without her help it would have been impossible for me to complete this book in such a short time. Dr. John Harvey and Dr. Ajaya Swami were kind enough to help during the revision and gave their valuable suggestions. We thank Nitya for word processing the manuscript, Darlene Clark for typesetting it, and Pat Schilt for proofreading it. Janet Lindgren did the layout. We acknowledge that Mr. P. K. Nijhawan's idea inspired us to write this book.

Sri Guru Gobind Singh
The tenth Sikh guru (1666–1708)

Sri Guru Nanak Dev
The first Sikh guru (1469–1539)

Introduction: History and Philosophy of Sikhism

As it was in the beginning: the Truth,
So always has it ever been: the Truth;
Likewise in the present is it: the Truth;
And throughout eternity shall it remain: the Truth.
—Guru Nanak Dev, *Japji*

Rarely in the annals of human history does there appear a personage capable of awakening the human heart's noblest virtues to such an extent that an entire nation dynamically expresses the finest of its inherent qualities. Guru Gobind Singh had such an exceptional personality. Matchless in character and unparalleled in attributes, striking in figure and divine in demeanor, he was the definitive warrior-saint. In battle he knew no equal; in piety he was sublime. His presence inspired awe, devotion, and valor. Poet, visionary, sage, warrior, and leader, he fearlessly rallied the valiant forces of righteousness lying dormant within the weary hearts of his people. The strength of his moral fiber and the conviction of his spiritual and social ideals inspired his nation to fulfill its noble destiny, uplifting it within a singular purpose. In the entire history of humankind, the unparalleled example of Guru Gobind Singh stands as a perennial source of inspiration for the leaders of the world.

The life of Guru Gobind Singh was strewn with innumerable hurdles to be overcome. In seventeenth century India, the Moguls, invaders from Asia Minor, were eroding and persecuting Indian civilization. The rajas*, with their tiny feudal estates, were egocentric and self-serving, providing only sporadic resistance to the alien intolerance. The Indian people had fallen into passive despondency due to the futility of individual action, and the mentality of the oppressed overrode the natural tendency to aspire and excel.

The Moguls, who had conquered the whole of northern India, had converted a large number of socially and economically deprived people to their religion, Islam*. The social injustices of foreign rule were oppressively apparent. Employment was limited to those who spoke Persian and practiced Islam; Koranic* laws and customs prevailed. Non-Muslims were treated as second class citizens, with few economic opportunities or civil liberties. Unfair taxes and restrictive laws were imposed upon them.

For lack of dynamic leadership and because the official state religion was Islam, Hindus could not unite, and they began to forget their noble heritage. People who wanted to devote their lives to intense spiritual practice went to secluded forest retreats and were not available to inspire or instruct householders. Racked by rigidity of thinking and heavily ritualized non-essential observances, the essence of the people's spiritual orientation started to become diluted and distorted. Their social values and spiritual practices yielded to prejudiced customs. Hindus, having lived under alien rule for almost a thousand years, became pessimistic, and their culture began to disintegrate. In addition, the country was being torn apart by sectarianism and religious fanaticism.

Such a society—one that is not systematized and organized, and does not remain vigilant—becomes a victim, and is finally helpless, leaving itself to blind destiny. Some of the noblest civilizations in the history of humanity have disappeared from the earth because of this negligent error. When such problems crept into the Indian social organization, making it incapable of self-defense, the Indian culture suffered. This phenomenal predicament was many-sided. First, it was a result of the innumerable castes, subcastes, and outcastes that divided Indian society into narrow segments. Second,the multiplicity of shrines with numerous gods and rigid rituals dissipated the strength of Indian society, for the communities did not unite under one roof. And third, Indian society was fractionated into hundreds of small feudal states, and there was no communication and cohesiveness. National integrity was thus hard to attain, and the Moguls had therefore been successful in invading India and becoming its rulers.

As a result of internal bickering and external domination, the entire fabric of Indian culture was in danger of degenerating into meaningless disparate remnants of its former glory. The Golden Bird that had been India was helplessly being tortured, and no champion had yet come forth to defend her.

In such desperate times, only a leader of heroic proportions is capable of meeting the difficult task presented by destiny. As the Bhagavad Gita (4.7-8) indicates, "Whenever dharma declines and the purpose of life is forgotten, [the Divine] manifests itself on earth . . . to protect the good, to destroy evil, and to reestablish dharma." In the seventeenth century Guru Gobind Singh reincarnated to uphold dharma in India.

Gross injustice imposed upon an entire populace creates such an imbalance in nature that the scales tip completely, lifting the opposite platform heavenward, thus bringing an avatar* earthward to confront the purveyor of evil and set the balance aright. Guru Gobind Singh was the heaven-sent solution to the terrible plight of Indian civilization during the cruel reign of Aurangzeb, the last powerful Mogul emperor.

The mantle of destiny fell early upon the capable shoulders of Guru Gobind Singh. He was in fact born to his mission, being the tenth and last in the Sikh guru lineage, which flourished during the sixteenth and seventeenth centuries. He was heir to the house of Sri Guru Nanak Dev, the founder of Sikh dharma and philosophy. Guru Nanak Dev (1469-1539) laid the foundation of Sikhism, expounding the gems of truth to be found in its sacred scripture, Sri Guru Granth Sahib, more commonly known as Adi Granth, or the First Book. This scripture is an anthology that contains the writings of seven of the Sikh gurus and thirteen other mystics from Hindu and Sufi* backgrounds who lived and wrote before the Sikh religion actually took institutional form. When Guru Gobind Singh (1666-1708) abolished the guru succession before his death, he designated his heir to be the Adi Granth, honoring the words of Guru Nanak Dev:

> The word of the guru is the music sublime;
> The word of the guru is the scripture divine;
> The word of the guru pervades beyond time.

His own writings were collected twenty years after his death and compiled as the Dasam Granth, the Book of the Tenth Master. It has two thousand verses and is considered to be one of the finest pieces of literature in Sikhism.

Guru Nanak Dev was determined to restore self-respect to a downtrodden and humiliated people and to transform the soul of an oppressed nation. He therefore created a practical, spiritual way of life. The Sikh heritage reminds the spiritual seeker of the social obligations of society—that the spiritual quest is not only vertical but horizontal as well. The affairs of human life are essential considerations to a spiritually aware individual. This conscientious responsibility to the practical aspects of mundane existence is fundamental to the spiritual practice of Sikhism. Sikhism represents an enlightened, logical expression from within the Indian heritage.

Guru Nanak Dev taught that the mosque and the temple are equal. He believed in the brotherhood of humankind and held the ideal of establishing harmonious relations between Hinduism and Islam. He embraced the universal principles of Hinduism and Sufism alike, thus synthesizing the two religious traditions. No formalism, rituals, superstitions, images, gods, castes, priesthoods, dogma, mortifications, inequalities, or intolerances are found in the teachings of Guru Nanak Dev.

Guru Nanak Dev refused to be lulled by the dull passivity of his times. He did not teach indifference but strove to realize his ideal regardless of the cost. He valued devotion and skillful action above renunciation and isolation, for his goal was the uplifting of the whole, not just a particular class or individual. Thus the hero, not the hermit, was held as the model for perfection. Social commitment was valued as highly as spiritual liberation.

The Sikh religion strives to create an ideal society that has as its basis spiritual awareness and ethical integrity. The householder who works hard to earn a livelihood and gives to the worthy is the true Sikh. Health and endurance of the body, mind, and spirit are equally maintained; moderation, purity, and selfless service are valued. Sikhism emphasizes the central unity of religions, accepting the great words of diverse spiritual teachers in a practical and synthesized way. Guru Nanak Dev said,

The throne of God exists in all places;
His treasure house fills up all spaces.
God, being Truth, lights up all faces.

Universal in acceptance and democratic in principle, the Sikh society strives to provide a wholesome, purposeful, and comfortable way of life in which people can effectively pursue their spiritual development. The excellence and utility of human life is honored and cultivated by providing proper education and building strong character.

In short, Sikhism expounds the ideal of a cultured person who lives holistically, with inner awareness of the Lord and with the purpose of serving the nation selflessly. Remembering the holy name of God in every breath of life and studying the sacred scripture are the major spiritual practices. Guru Nanak Dev said, "Harkening to the Name bestows truth, divine wisdom, contentment." Sikhism believes in one God—formless, eternal, infinite, all-pervading, absolute, beyond the comprehension of the human mind. Truth, or Reality, can be attained by grace through devotion, righteousness, and selfless service. This is similar to the teachings of Vedanta*, the last and finest part of the Vedas. The guru is the indwelling divinity who shows the way of self-surrender to God.

Guru Nanak Dev said, "To be saved, live according to the Truth. Keep no feeling of animosity for anyone. God resides in every bosom. Forgiveness is love at its highest power. Where there is forgiveness there is God Himself." A great monotheist and humanist, he advocated equality, devotion, and service as principal tenets of his path. He valued ahimsa, non-harming, as a guideline for action, instructing his followers to practice it in this way:

Do not wish evil for anyone. This is ahimsa of thought.
Do not speak harshly of anyone. This is ahimsa of speech.
Do not obstruct anyone's work. This is ahimsa of action.
If a man speaks ill of you, forgive him.
Practice physical, mental, and spiritual endurance.
Help the suffering even at the cost of your life.

In his youth Guru Nanak Dev, the son of Hindu parents who lived near Lahore, sought out the company of wandering hermits before establishing himself in the life of a householder. Even then he remained preoccupied with spiritual matters, studying the bhakti (devotional) literature, especially the writings of Kabir, several Vaishnava* saints, and the Sufi mystics. After thirty years he dedicated himself full time to spirituality, traveling with two disciples, Bala and Mardana, from Assam to Mecca and from Tibet to Ceylon. He finally settled in Kartapur, where he resumed the householder's life in an exemplary way. The last fifteen years of his life were spent teaching his disciples. The universality and vitality of his teachings revived the true essence of spirituality in India.

Guru Nanak Dev instituted the lineage of gurus by designating his disciple Sri Angad Dev (1504-1552) as his successor, thereby disregarding his own son, who believed in the path of renunciation and ascetic practices. Sri Angad Dev devised the Gurmukhi script, established the tradition of shared community meals, and built temples (*gurudwaras*) from which the teachings could be spread. He chose his elderly disciple Sri Amar Das (1479-1574), a great reformer, to succeed him as the third guru. Guru Amar Das organized the Sikhs by establishing twenty-two dioceses and appointing officials to represent them. He helped improve the position of women by abolishing *purdah* (veiling) and *sati pratha* (self-immolation of widows). He made communal dining of all his followers mandatory, without any discrimination of caste, creed, or color. He was succeeded by his son-in-law Guru Ram Das (1534-1581), founder of the holy city of Amritsar.

Guru Ram Das' youngest son Sri Arjan Dev (1563-1606), the fifth guru, made Amritsar a place of pilgrimage by installing there the Adi Granth, which he compiled and to which he contributed. He built many temples throughout the Punjab, including the Golden Temple (Harmandir) in Amritsar. To support these projects, he began the tradition of receiving annual tithes of love offerings from the followers. Guru Arjan Dev took the principles set down by Guru Nanak Dev and with them founded the religion and organized the community known as Sikhs—that is, "selfless servers." The Mogul emperor, concerned about Guru Arjan Dev's increasing power, accused him of vilifying Islam. The emperor finally had the Guru tortured and executed, thereby making him the first Sikh martyr and setting a Sikh precedent for self-sacrifice for the sake of dharma.

In response to the Mogul intolerance, Guru Arjan Dev's son, Guru Har Govind (1595-1644), channeled the Sikh desire to regain the prestige and dignity of the people by uniting them through training in arms. He was persecuted for this, but the shift in emphasis took hold, and disciplined valor became characteristic of the Sikh disciples, who rallied devotedly around their guru and became the defenders of dharma. His successor, Sri Har Rai (1630-1661), continued to acquire arms and train warriors to repel tyranny and injustice. He considered this to be a natural aspect of his spiritual office. The role of a warrior became the Sikh ideal of vigorous ethical service to the community in defense of a just cause. Sri Har Rai's young son, Sri Harkishan (1656-1664), served only three years, and despite his youth sagaciously selected a worthy and deserving successor, Sri Teg Bahadur (1621-1675), bypassing several closer relations to do so.

Guru Teg Bahadur, the ninth guru, son of Guru Har Govind, was a wise and strong leader who had lived in seclusion for a long time before assuming leadership. He then traveled broadly to convey the Sikh teachings throughout the country. He founded Anandpur in the Shivalik Hills, which provided a more secure position than did the plains surrounding Amritsar. He was also a poet, as had been the first five gurus. He fathered Gobind Rai, who was to become Guru Gobind Singh, the last and most glorious Sikh guru. During Guru Teg Bahadur's reign, the Hindu pandits* and brahmins,* persecuted by the cruel Mogul emperor Aurangzeb, appealed to the guru for protection. Concerned about the escalating intolerance of the Mogul forces, Guru Teg Bahadur exclaimed,

> "The ways of dharma we must defend.
> The rulers' oppression must reach its end.
> Someone should prepare to offer his life
> To rid the earth of their evil and strife!"

His young son, Gobind, who admired his father tremendously, eagerly offered,

"None could be worthier, it is true,
For such a noble act than you!"

Deeply touched by the wisdom and bravery of his son's reply, the guru sent a message to the Mogul court stating that if the guru could be persuaded to accept Islam, all the others would also, but if not, they would all maintain their age-old dharma. The emperor, who had sworn to exterminate all religions except Islam, interpreted the note as a request for persecution and death, to which he responded by bringing the guru to Delhi as a prisoner. When faced with the alternative of choosing Islam or death, Guru Teg Bahadur embraced death, stating, "I give my head but not my honor!" His martyrdom united the people in the cause of dharma.

The severed head of Guru Teg Bahadur, lying where it had fallen, was taken away under the cloak of a stormy night by a courageous and devoted disciple. The relic was reverently delivered to the young Sikh heir, Guru Gobind Singh, who accepted the tragedy with matchless fortitude and presence. Though only nine years of age, the guru, by virtue of his innate nobility and wisdom, was already well-suited to assume the spiritual sovereignty of the Sikhs.

If a writer of adventure novels attempted to create the ultimate tale of chivalry and daring, he could not surpass the real-life story of Guru Gobind Singh. Adventure-story heroics pale in comparison to his feats. His amazing exploits could thrill the imagination of any young boy, and his noble tenderness of sentiment melt the heart of any young girl. His was a refined and well-rounded personality, versed in the subtleties of culture and warfare and steeped in the depths of spirituality.

Guru Gobind Singh designed his youthful years at Anandpur to be a time of assiduous practice and training as preparation for his destiny. Adept in warfare, contemplation, hunting, study, and poetry, he instilled in his people confidence in themselves and their leader. In archery, horsemanship, and swordplay, he excelled. His love of knowledge was profound and his intellect keen. A voracious student of India's great philosophical and spiritual literature, he assured its dissemination and preservation through translations and libraries. He found inexplicable solace in the beauty of nature, regularly turning to some solitary retreat to replenish his spirit and commune with the melodious wisdom of streams. The writing of poetry was his sacred passion, and his range of expression was broad. He showed mastery in every meter and every mood, and in many languages. The verve and vigor of his poetry convey the rhythm and feeling of battle as no other, and its beauty delicately expresses the depths of spirituality.

His court was the seat of poetry as well as the sponsor of daily hunting expeditions. These the guru relished with skill that was later to show itself in his talent as a battle strategist. Despite his military brilliance, he was a lover of peace, and he followed a death-defying code of ethics. He never struck the first blow, attacked the enemy, or took territory, and he always forgave penitents, honored his word, and assisted worthy supplicants. His profound devotion to the one universal Lord and his compassion for humanity were apparent throughout his life, for he determined at an early age to dedicate every breath of his existence to the steadfast preservation of truth and virtue.

He guided his spiritual community with a conviction and compassion that won their dedicated devotion. He built up his royal court and armed forces, and uplifted the spirits of his people with his heroic and spiritual poems. He also installed a massive drum in Anandpur, which was sounded daily to excite the community's heart to valor, to call them to communal meals, and to announce the hunt. Anandpur became a model city filled with the fervor and compassion that the shared purpose of the people generated.

A few of the petty rajas of the surrounding hills, however, were filled with envy and schemed against the guru. To reduce their hostile unrest, Guru Gobind Singh left Anandpur, accepting an invitation to visit the nearby estate of a friendly raja. There he set upon the task of founding a new city, nestled upon the banks of the Yamuna River. It was called Paonta, and there he resumed his life of spiritual and martial training and literary pursuit.

In Paonta flourished his poetic genius, beautifully expressing all sides of his glorious nature. His poetic rapture was sublime. While composing one poem, he was transported into ecstasy for sixteen hours simply by contemplating the words "Thou art That." In his poetry of valor, which resounded with chivalry and devotion, he referred to God as a sword of protection, and he praised the goddess Durga as a source of shakti* and the upholder of dharma. He honored valiant death in holy battle as a noble and worthy end. During his three-year stay Paonta became a prominent center of Sikh cultural and spiritual regeneration.

From the time Guru Gobind Singh was twenty-three, the wheel of destiny swept him into events that compelled him to fulfill his purpose. Some of the emperor's feudal vassals, still enraged by the guru's noble presence in their midst, were jealous and antagonistic. They plotted against him and attacked him six miles from Paonta at Bhangani. The guru's troops, filled with devotion and dedicated to the sword as a sacred upholder of justice, defeated the unrighteous enemy in the raging fury of battle. The aggressors quickly learned deep respect for the Sikh heart and sword.

The guru meant harm to no one and held no territorial ambitions, yet he found himself surrounded by prejudice and antagonism. He said, "I have no animosity toward anyone. I want only to be left in peace and to propagate the cause of dharma. My father gave his head to protect dharma, and I live for the same cause. But here am I, trying to infuse a new spirit in an injured civilization, being refused cooperation."

Returning to Anandpur, he continued to establish an ideal community based on sacrifice for the cause of dharma. He stoked the fires of righteousness and nationalism to elevate his people to the heights of positive fervor for social and spiritual victory. Each Sikh was free, equal, self-reliant, confident, and eager to offer his life for the cause of dharma.

The guru continued composing dynamic verse of valor and spirit and perfecting the Sikh community. Three of his four sons were also born during this ten-year period, and he brought them up to embody the Sikh ideal. Anandpur and the Sikh community grew ever stronger, for the guru's followers responded to his service, love, and leadership with the conviction of purposeful devotion.

The guru's zeal inspired an increase in the annual offerings given by all Sikhs on Baisaki (New Year's Day). In response, the guru reformed the system for collection, divesting the local tithe collectors, thus abolishing the bureaucratic hierarchy that had kept his followers from direct contact with him. Sikhs from all around now visited him at Anandpur annually, and his fame as a warrior-saint spread, attracting many chivalrous youths as well as poets and spiritual seekers.

In 1699 the Sikhs were given opportunity to demonstrate their dedication to their guru and their mission. On Baisaki, when all the Sikhs gathered together at Anandpur, the guru showed the depths of his daring, free-thinking, and determination to awaken his people to their full potential. He boldly addressed the assembly, exclaiming, "My sword today wants a head! Let any one of my true Sikhs come forward. Is there not one Sikh of mine who would sacrifice his life?" The shocked audience froze in numb stillness. Again the guru declared his request. Then from the mute gathering a humble voice called, "My head is at thy disposal, O my true Lord. There could be no greater gain than dying by thy sword!"

The guru took the faithful disciple to a ceremonial tent and returned with blood-drenched sword to demand another head. The pleas of his mother and advisors could not dissuade the determined guru, and four more noble devotees offered their heads to the guru's sword before he at last relented.

Then the crowd's bewilderment quickly turned into relieved shock when the guru emerged from the tent accompanied by all five volunteers, clad in ceremonial warrior garb. The Five Beloved Ones, the Panj Piare,* had passed the ultimate test and were declared to be the foundation upon which the Khalsa, the new order, would be formed. The guru initiated them with *amrit** (nectar), sword-stirred water from a steel chalice. Then he told them to accept the five insignia of the new order: sword, steel wristband, fighting breeches, unshorn hair, and a comb to keep their hair kempt. Guru Gobind Singh declared that all Sikhs were from that moment to be known by the surname Singh, meaning "lion." He told the community, "I name you the Khalsa. You shall keep forever the flame of life lit in you, unflickering, in constant prayer to the timeless Being. In each of you shall the whole brotherhood be incarnated. You are my sons, both in flesh and spirit. One who serves humanity selflessly pleases me. Nothing else is pleasing to my mind. I am exalted because you have exalted me. My possessions, my body, my soul are at the disposal of my people. For nothing else avails." He then requested the Five to initiate him also, thereby demonstrating his democratic philosophy. "I have made Khalsa the guru!" he exclaimed.

Many thousands were initiated into the new order that very day, and Sikhism entered a challenging new phase. The creation of the Khalsa was the culmination of two hundred years of social and spiritual awakening wrought by the ten Sikh gurus. The disheartened people had been vibrantly transformed into a community of stouthearted spiritual warriors.

The intolerant emperor Aurangzeb, busy with his campaigns in the south, was alarmed to hear of the Guru's rapidly growing power and devoted following. The Moguls therefore began attacking the Sikhs, who responded boldly, inflicting a severe defeat upon the Moguls. But the hard-won peace was short-lived. The next five years at Anandpur saw an endless series of skirmishes and sporadic battles in which the hill lords joined forces with the emperor's troops. The Sikhs responded to the hostility with skill and bravery, as Anandpur suffered repeated assaults by the Moguls. Finally, in 1705, the enemy laid siege on the city, determined to cut off supplies and starve the Sikhs into submission.

The hardship on the Sikhs was severe. Night raids outside the city gates to procure supplies required a group of men to fetch goods and a group to die in assuring their safe return. The privations became so intense that the guru could no longer allow his people to suffer so. When the enemy offered safe conduct for the guru, his family, his troops, and his goods, the guru finally agreed to surrender and evacuate the city. To demonstrate his awareness of his enemy's true nature, however, the guru first sent forth bundles of refuse, upon which the greedy enemy troops fell with enthusiasm, expecting treasures of gold and jewels. Sure of the enemy's murderous intent, the guru secreted away his mother and two younger sons, hidden by the cover of night. Then with about five hundred troops, led by himself, his two older sons, and the Five Beloveds, he left Anandpur. Thus the great humanitarian warrior-saint turned from the site of his dream's fruition, never to gaze upon it again.

As soon as the guru's troops had left the city, the enemy rushed to surround them, disregarding all promises of safe departure. Many valiant Sikh warriors died that night, and the entire group was scattered. The guru, his two older sons, and about forty Sikhs were able to make a fort of a mud house in Chamkaur. The massive enemy horde swarmed around the house that sheltered the tiny Sikh force, and an epic battle began.

There the guru witnessed the valiant deaths of his two teenage sons, who delighted his heart with their daring and skill, even in the face of certain death. There the last five surviving Sikhs imposed upon their guru their right of vote—insisting that he escape at night, taking the only chance for life that remained. Thereby was the noble guru reduced to being a fugitive in his own country, and thereby was he saved to reinstate the Khalsa.

The guru's mother and his two younger sons, who had entrusted themselves to the protection of their guide, were betrayed. The innocents were handed over to the Mogul governor of Sarhind, where the glory of their noble characters was to be immortalized. The cruel *nawab**, Wazir Khan, imprisoned the children and forced them to select Islam or death. One of the boys replied, "None can force us to abjure the faith of our forefathers. We shall forfeit our lives but not our honor. This worldly authority is not everlasting. The enemy will prove its own ruin." The heartless nawab ordered the boys to be bricked up in a wall, but still they did not yield. Finally, the nawab had them executed.

The guru, after many adventures, found temporary refuge in the village home of a devoted disciple. He listened to the tragic account of his younger sons' deaths with perfect composure, and praised God for receiving again into His divine embrace that which was already His. Yet the guru swore to destroy the tyrannous empire and thereby preserve dharma. He wrote an "Epistle of Victory" to the Emperor Aurangzeb in which he condemned the emperor for his treacherous breach of faith in the evacuation of Anandpur and for the cruel deaths of his young sons.

The guru quickly gathered more troops, including many thousands of new initiates. Encamped near the desert oasis of Muktsar he addressed them, saying, "My message of hope must spread from one corner of this land to the other. I cannot sit back and relax when my nation is at stake." Some naive followers proposed that he make a truce with the emperor, to which the guru replied, "I make no compromise with intolerance and tyranny." He reminded them of the noble lineage of martyrs who had offered their lives to defeat the forces of adharma and invited them to vindicate justice by following him. They responded heartily and prepared for battle. The Sikh army stood fast against the spirited Mogul charge at Muktsar, at last forcing the Moguls to retire.

Great valor and sacrifice were required for that victory, and almost every Sikh warrior was slain, including a group of forty penitent Sikhs who had returned, having renounced the guru before the evacuation of Anandpur.

Undaunted by his losses, the guru embarked on a journey to spread the teachings of Guru Nanak Dev. Those who heard his liberating message were inspired to follow his dynamic teachings. He found the southern Punjab well-suited to his work, as its secluded oasis and jungles were far from Mogul troops, and its freedom-loving, hard-working people felt privileged to receive his teaching. He settled there, creating a new city called Damdama. Many people gathered there, and it became a hub of activity and inspiration and a seat of learning. More than one hundred thousand people were inspired to join the Khalsa order at Damdama. Here the guru enjoyed a period of peace during which he recompiled the Adi Granth.

During this time the emperor Aurangzeb had become seriously ill. Bedridden and facing death, he feared the consequences of having tormented a holy man. Finally he dictated a reply to the guru's Letter of Victory, requesting a meeting of reconciliation. Unaware of this, the guru, hearing of the emperor's failing health, set out on the arduous journey to meet him. En route, he received word of the emperor's death.

The three sons of Aurangzeb, all claimants to the throne, commenced the habitual Mogul disputes of succession. The eldest, Muazzam, had the best claim and, unlike his father, was a broadminded, liberal man. To attain his goal, he beseeched the guru's aid and blessings. As the house of Nanak never refused a worthy supplicant, the guru honored the request, sending some troops to assist him in battle. Muazzam thereby won the title.

Despite the friendly terms of their leaders, some Mogul and Sikh soldiers could not forget their former animosity, and incidents of violence occurred. In addition, the emperor, though grateful for the guru's help and respectful of his station and teachings, did little to honor the guru's request that he quell the tyrannies of fanatics such as Nawab Wazir Khan of Sarhind, who had executed the guru's young sons. Their parleys therefore ceased, and the guru went his own way.

It was at this point, in 1708, that the guru went to Nander, on the banks of the Godavari River, where he was to meet an ascetic monk named Bairagi Madho Das. The guru found the hermit's hut unoccupied and made himself at home, resting upon the monk's cot. When the renunciate spied the interloper, he rushed to his hut with the intention of ousting him, but when his eyes met those of the guru he fell in supplication at his feet, declaring himself the guru's follower.

It is said that the guru/disciple relationship is the most sacred of all. "When the disciple is ready, the guru appears" is a true saying. The ancient bond of disciple and guru brought these two together at the most opportune time, for the ascetic had formerly been a *kshatriya** (warrior), and his battle skills were to be greatly needed by the guru.

The hermit Bairagi Madho Das had been known as Lachman Dev before he was ordained as a monk. He had been born to a family of Rajput farmers in Jammu in 1670. As a boy he enjoyed archery and hunting; as a youth he established a reputation for having great skill in wielding arms. He also had a sensitive heart, for his whole life changed because of the tender feelings he experienced during an incident that occurred one day while he was hunting. He had shot a deer, but when he came to inspect his kill, he saw that his arrow had ripped open the womb of a doe, revealing two unborn fawns lying dead in their mother's blood. The sight filled him with a revulsion for killing. Moved to an acute awareness of life's transitory and sorrowful nature, he instantly decided to take up the life of a renunciate.

The young seeker, still in his teens, began to wander in search of peace and meaning. He encountered various *sadhus** (holy men) and was eventually ordained by one in Kasur, becoming a *bairagi** (monk) called Madho Das. After a while he left there and wandered to Nander. There he became the disciple of a Nath sadhu*, renowned for yogic *siddhis** (psychic powers). Practicing a life of meditation and disciplined asceticism, he became an accomplished yogi*. He was so advanced that he was appointed his teacher's successor, heading the hermitage and helping those who came to him for blessings and guidance. After his debate with Guru Gobind Singh, however, he left the life of a hermit to take up action in the world in the defense of dharma. Thus was he initiated with amrit, given the name Banda Singh Bahadur, and assigned to lead the guru's mission.

Guru Gobind Singh trained his new disciple carefully, and Banda's skill encouraged the guru's hopes for establishing freedom and justice. But the Nawab of Sarhind, wary of the emperor's conciliatory treatment of the guru, was afraid and jealous. The emperor's growing sympathy for the guru's view made the nawab fear that the emperor might attack the nawab to avenge the deaths of the guru's sons. The nawab therefore plotted the guru's assassination, sending two of his trusted men to infiltrate the guru's camp at Nander. One day, as the guru reclined after prayers, one of the assassins, having just taken *prasad** (food) from the Guru's own hand, brutally thrust a dagger into the guru's chest, nearly piercing his heart. Again the assassin struck, but before he could inflict a third blow, the wounded guru slashed off the assailant's head with his saber. The Sikhs rushing into the gory scene swiftly dispatched the other assassin and immediately looked to the health of the wounded guru.

An expert surgeon was able to mend the gashing wounds, and the guru was beginning to heal. The sedentary life of a recuperating patient was foreign to the guru's nature, however, and he rapidly tried to resume his normal activities. While he was stretching a large bow one day, the wound reopened and bled profusely. The guru's physical frame, the worn veteran of countless battles, was weakened beyond recovery by this traumatic relapse, and the guru knew the end of his mortal life was near.

He prepared himself for his final transition by instructing his followers to abide always in cheerfulness and never give way to mourning. Knowing it was time to name a successor, he bade them bring to him the Sri Granth Sahib and declared, "This is my commandment: install Sri Granth Sahib in my place. He who acknowledges it will obtain his reward. The guru will rescue him. Know this as the truth." Thus he discontinued the personal guru lineage and assured the Sikhs of consistent, wise guidance throughout the centuries. By declaring the Adi Granth as guru, he made the guru lineage everlasting: the word would survive, and the Khalsa would follow its message.

The guru then dressed himself in full battle array, bravely mounted his favorite blue-grey steed, and bidding farewell to his troops, rode to a ceremonial tent, where he enjoyed an evening of peaceful solitude before casting off the weary garment of his body and meeting the Eternal.

Left with the Khalsa and the Adi Granth, the Sikhs found a source of inner inspiration to guide them. The guru actually permeated the collective unconscious of the community and thereby continued to shape the course of their noble endeavors in the cause of human dignity and prestige. Banda Singh Bahadur also served them for eight years as the spearhead of the Sikh mission, firmly opposing the injustice and tyranny of the Mogul governors.

As a leader, Banda Bahadur was outstanding and unique. His wisdom, zeal, and humanitarian love enhanced his remarkable skill in wielding arms. Warriors rallied to his battle cry with enthusiastic determination. His keen battle strategies and uncommon positive will brought him victory when none seemed possible. For three years he knew no defeat at all, and during the time he battled the Moguls he turned the tide so forcefully that they could never again reign over the Sikh community. But in so doing he incurred the intense wrath of Mogul bigotry, and they plotted to lay siege to him. He was thereby cut off and was made captive in December 1715.

The Moguls locked Banda Bahadur in a strong iron cage bound atop an elephant and carried him to Delhi by slow procession. The two-month display of his captivity was designed to subdue the Sikhs' zeal, but the sight of their beloved hero so mistreated actually stoked the fire of their determination.

The Mogul cruelty knew no bounds as they prepared the warrior-saint for martyrdom before the people of Delhi. Placing his young son in his lap, they forced the two to choose Islam or death. Banda Bahadur kissed his son, saying, "I am happy you are leaving the world before me, because I will have no fear of your ever embracing Islam. You are following the tradition of the young sons of Guru Gobind Singh, who are waiting for you to join them." The barbaric Moguls then tore the boy's body into shreds, placing a garland of his intestines around his father's neck and forcing the boy's bleeding heart into his mouth. During this atrocity, the entire assembly wept, but Banda Bahadur himself remained tranquil. Then the evil torturers began the father's slow execution by piercing his eyes with red-hot spikes.

Banda Bahadur's martyrdom fueled the people's resolve to continue the mission of the gurus. A series of Sikh generals sustained the impetus established by the valiant accomplishments of Banda Bahadur. Finally they drove the Moguls from their land, and never again did Mogul power threaten dharma in the hub of Sikh influence.

The Sikh ideal established by Guru Gobind Singh constituted a resurrection of the national character of India, which had been buried under centuries of oppressive foreign rule. Guru Gobind Singh aroused the dynamic quality of deep purpose and self-respect inherent in his people's psyche. He united the people in the spirit of tolerance, humanitarian concern, and excellence that was their essential nature. Banda Bahadur carried on the dynamic crusade of Guru Gobind Singh, and within a century other Sikh leaders established a free and secure society in which the people could thrive materially and spiritually.

The confident action and universal outlook of Sikhism took root in the Indian spirit due to the bold and insightful efforts of Guru Gobind Singh. The ideal Sikh society, which values a cooperative, purposeful, and egalitarian perspective, provides a model for social and spiritual progress. The Sikh outlook can rouse the dormant potentials of a vanquished personality or a vanquished nation.

Guru Gobind Singh's dynamic philosophy is universally appealing and democratic. It rallies the spirit to proper action, just as he aroused the spirit of his disciple Banda in the famous dialogue of destiny they enjoyed just one month before the guru's death. The dialogue between Guru Gobind Singh and Banda Singh Bahadur took place in circumstances similar to those of the great dialogue between Krishna and Arjuna, which is recorded in the Srimad Bhagavad Gita. The purpose of both dialogues is to inspire the disciple to uphold dharma and attain spiritual fulfillment. The message of Guru Gobind Singh is universal, uplifting, and based upon the practical expression of divine love. Its essence is as relevant today as it was in his time, for the dharma always needs to be upheld.

> I have surrendered my mind, heart, and soul to God.
> I am the smallest instrument of God.
> I will pay homage to no one but God.
> I will not follow any tradition but Truth, which is God.
> I am a messenger who will deliver the message of God.
> I will lovingly sow the seeds of the pure love of God.
>
> —Guru Gobind Singh, *Bachitra Natak*

1

The Drama of Life

'Tis from the East the sun does rise,
And from the East do dawn the wise.
That spiritual region has been the home
From which great saints and prophets roam,
And India's womb has given birth
To sages of unbounded worth.
Thus in the Punjab was there born
A sage whose life to Truth was sworn.
Sri Guru Nanak was his name,
And universal grew his fame.
His life was blesséd from the first,
For had he an uncommon thirst
For Truth and for the life divine
And with God's his own heart entwine.
He had a job, a home, wife—
He cherished well householder's life.
He brought up children in the world
While in his heart divine thoughts swirled.
He reached high spiritual dignity
And served man always with benignity.
Teaching the path of pure service and love,
He showed men the way to awareness above.
People of all paths did love and revere him.

His selfless outlook to their hearts endeared him.
He was universal, beyond place and time.
His method was skillful, his message sublime.
He deeply inspired the people and brought them
To join each other within all he taught them.
His students, called Sikhs, are to his teachings true.
They live by the words of their revered guru.
He was the first of the ten; and the last
Was Sri Guru Gobind, whose wisdom was vast.
Gobind was an avatar; Truth was his mission.
He upheld the dharma, and his life's fruition
Was to fulfill what Nanak Dev taught long before
So all could have peace and thus help others more.

All the Sikh gurus taught love in action,
Accepting all, excluding no faction.
They respected their freedom and honored the right
Of people to find their own way to the Light.
They taught that when dharma begins to erode,
The righteous must rally and carry the load.
Their purpose is always to maintain the force
That flows down to man from the ultimate Source.
Through selfless service the Sikhs do sustain
The balance that dharma must always retain
To keep the good strong and keep evil at bay,
To live out their lives in a virtuous way.

They watch the times and stay aware
So they'll be able to prepare
To herald each new challenge lurking
Within the future's untold working.
When precious values are at stake
Each moment could the difference make.
When nation suffers rebirth's throes,
Time measures all its hopes and woes.
And each year marks the cycle's turn

Of one more chance for men to learn
That destiny rests in their hands,
And not in whim of wind or sands.
From Truth do hark the venerable masters
Who guide us far from life's disasters
And teach by words and by their deeds
What every yearning spirit needs:
To know that we immortal be
And of one God the devotee,
That we are children of the Sun
That shines the Light on all and one,
And hither do we all embark
To play our role and find the spark
That glows within from one and all,
Despite their evil or their gall.

Life's drama we as players render;
To Playwright's will do we surrender.
And we, those scripted for the saga,
Play one note in the eternal raga.
We act, we feel, for a short time;
Mere shadows do our lives but mime.
Beyond gray figures in myriad poses,
Ensnared in webs, the mystery closes.
Yet the true Source shines ever bright.
The drama of life pales at the sight
That the Timeless within mere time does dwell,
And imperfect is but Perfection's shell.
The Timeless resides in life, low to high,
From first eager gasp to last muted sigh.
The Timeless alone is immune to time's throes;
All else is but subject to life's tugs and blows.
And we, in the midst of our shallow drama,
Pay tribute to our inner core, called Brahma.
Truth's network springs forth from within our own essence
And holds us in pattern of dharma's quintessence.

We are its subject; we are its master.
And of its web we make peace or disaster.

Life's panorama is varied and vast.
Its Painter chose man as head of the cast.
Watching the tableau of amazing events,
Of soaring achievements this drama presents,
One sees rich traditions set in the design
Laden with highlights of valor that shine
Amid glorious legends and bright noble faces
Depicting the zeniths of all climes and races.
But rarest among these—the rarest of rare—
Is the man of dharma, to whom none compare.
Such were the gurus, such was Sri Gobind—
Men who were from their beginning predestined
To convey the meaning of God's beautiful code,
To decipher its portent and reveal the road
By which the great race of Bharata* can show
That the grace of God in its veins does flow.

O Guru Gobind! the time is now
When to thee must we all avow
To set the course of events straight
That have by narrow rails of hate
Been upset from their destination
And hit upon a culmination
That calls for divine intervention
Beyond the human comprehension.
For men to dharma have been untrue
And must suffer pangs that thus accrue.
They by their lack of vision belie
That they have led the plan awry,
And so we must at last now plead
That thou wilt send with all due speed
Some spark of light to this ancient land
Where we in painful conflict stand,

Incurring hurt upon our brothers,
That God's sweet favor 'pon us smothers.
O thou, who Bharat loved and blest,
O thou, who from her foes did wrest
Her noble virtue and one true home,
Make to us now thy guidance known!
Oh, let men dharma's way see right!
The heaven-born pale at the sight
Of unjust acts in name of dharma
Wrought by those ensnared in karma.

Where are the Aryans—men of yore
Who could by their bold hearts restore
Their homeland's grandeur and assure
Her rightful place; who could endure
The empty taunts and unkind jeers;
Whose noble hearts are free of fears
And pounding with desire to live
In peace, with love and work to give?
The India that we adore
Needs those bright ones who can restore
The ancient lineage of her beauty
And rally to their rightful duty.
Who will carry out this mission?
Who'll help manifest this vision?
In service of community,
In answer to their destiny—
We need people steeped in dharma
To help us break the bonds of karma*—
Ones who can our hearts inspire
To live for what we do aspire.

To help the people stay on track,
To their great men let them look back.
Oh, let the people happily sing
A tale to make their spirits ring.

Let them sing of Bahadur,
For in him Truth shines ever pure.
And let them tell of Gobind Singh,
Who many men to God did bring.
Let them sing so they don't falter;
Let their Text become their psalter
In which they its true wisdom find
To know the path they should unwind
To ascend steadfast to their calling,
And progress foot-sure without falling.

They should hear of that fateful day
When two great heroes had their say,
When they in great debate did wage
A talk between adept and sage.
For Banda, the beloved seeker,
Was lost and was becoming weaker.
When such sincere ones lose their way
Truth's words alone can then them sway,
And so did guru search him out
To dispel all his fear and doubt,
And set him on the path aright
To blaze the trail up to the height
Where men of dharma live in peace,
Where love prevails and conflicts cease.

That great auspicious interaction
Brought Banda's soul deep satisfaction,
For then he understood the way
That soul in Truth can ever stay
While serving man with selfless spirit.
It is now told for all to hear it.
Through dialogue great truths are shown:
Now through this one let peace be known!
So let it in our hearts now ring, and may it long endure—
The song of Guru Gobind Singh and Banda Bahadur!

2

The Meeting

The sacred Godavari meanders by
Where Rama and Sita used to lie
On its lush banks in forest's grove
Where yogis ripe with wisdom rove,
Performing their austerity,
Retaining for posterity
The sacred teachings of the sages
That men have cherished through the ages.
On these historic holy banks,
One sadhu lives among their ranks
Who warrior turned a recluse is—
A soldier who embraced truces
To take upon himself the training
Of those who live with freedom reigning.
Renounced he all he had before,
Surrendered all forevermore,
Having come to see his life
As adding to man's human strife,
After having killed a doe
Whose womb ripped open, there to show
Two tiny fawns, dead—without breath.
Before their life, they met their death.
The poignant shock of such a sight

Turned warrior's heart against all fight.
In that pathetic, touching scene
Of babes and mother so serene
In horror's fatal final grasp,
Did he his sword and sheath unclasp,
And vowed he ne'er again to cause
So vile a crime 'gainst nature's laws.

So turned he to the hermit's life,
Forsaking wealth and job and wife,
In search of inner harmony
And answers to cosmogony.
Thus did Bairagi Madho Das
Place himself where his path would cross
With one who knew that which he sought.
And from that moment he was caught,
By destiny and by his love,
And hence was guided from above.
So did Bairagi to woods recourse
To cleanse his heart and find the Source.

Despite his resolution bold
His heart could never be consoled.
His practices had come to naught.
Though with sincerity he sought
To purify his inner anguish,
The worthy yogi yet did languish.
Atop even the highest peak
Contentment did he ever seek.
He seemed to be a placid river,
But underneath his heart did quiver,
For conflict in his mind remained,
His warrior nature kept restrained
As he pursued ascetic rigor
And contemplated life with vigor.

Then comes the long-awaited day
When destiny would have its way.
Omens flit and flutter by;
Stars pose rightly in the sky.
Paces he now up, now down—
At first a smile and then a frown.
His mind is scattered, then composed;
Nothing is as he supposed.
And why has he brought out his sword?
It seems to be a sign untoward.

Beyond the grove the armies camp;
The air sends sound of footfalls' tramp.
The soldiers prepare for the day—
Some clean their weapons; others pray.
Their guru then rides into sight
Just as the dawn breaks through the night.
The Divine presses through the veil to the known,
And thus are his wonder and grandeur so shown.
Unconquered and holy, he rides on his steed.
Both yogi and warrior, he has but one need:
For all men in justice and freedom to live,
And to Truth their lives and their efforts to give.
The goddess of Truth is the sword that he wields;
Her power surrounds him—bright halos it yields.
And Shiva, destroyer who lords over time,
Protects him with armor strong-built and sublime.

The hermit hears the war drum's sound,
And in his heart feelings abound;
Impinging 'pon his holy haven
A shadow of his past—engraven
Still within his warrior's heart
As hermit's life he did take part—
Comes bursting forth into his mind.
Can he from pain keep himself blind?

For as he prays and makes oblations,
Do others lie in harsh privations.
Can he have made the right selection:
To hide away? Some predilection
Begins to dawn within him now.
Should he rescind his hermit's vow?
That life that yielded spiritual rapture,
That gentle, peaceful life, did capture
His weary, war-torn, world-tossed spirit
And prompted him stay ever near it,
To keep at bay life's cruel action
And countermand dissatisfaction.
The restlessness creeps up again
That first he felt on that day when
He forsook all that he held dear.
But stop! These doubts he can't dare hear.
He knows his is the perfect way:
The sages do it homage pay.
So cease this useless wavering
The die is cast—stop quavering.

The sudden sound of conch's blow
Does in his heart a feeling sow,
And quick he turns to catch a glance
Of someone at his hut's entrance.
He rushes down to roust him out
But sees his face and falls devout
At those fine precious holy feet
That he had hoped one day to meet.
'Twas Guru Gobind—the greatest one
Of whom the soul and nation sung,
Who molded men with a new fire,
Men whom Bairagi did admire:
Men of action and inner calm
Who soothe the world with divine balm,
Men of valor and noble bearing

Yet simple, kind, and ever-caring,
Men in whom the spirit glows
And in whom guru's guidance shows.
Each dignified in his demeanor
And disciplined to make him keener,
Soldiers who are calm in action,
Who radiate sublime attraction,
Who find retreat in their heart's shrine
Through inner peace and love divine.

The guru found Bairagi's place
And came to meet him face to face.
Bairagi, who had turned away,
Was searched out, to his own doorway.
And when he strove to give *pranams**
Was lifted up by guru's arms
And held there in intense embrace
As hearts did lifetimes then retrace—
The guru and belov'd disciple
Held in friendship archetypal.
In silent union without voice
Did inwardly their hearts rejoice
To meet in flesh again at last
And proceed onward from the past.
Then sit they down to there transpire
Sacred exchange of holy fire,
When guru sets at complete ease
Disciple's doubts, like soothing breeze.
As guru makes himself at home
Disciple opens up the tome
Of secret unsolved conflicts held
Deep within his heart unquelled.

3

Guru and Disciple

Thus said Banda:
O Guru, what wonder transpires—
What strange fate or strong force conspires—
That thou, august and holy one,
Should honor this unworthy son
With thy kind presence and great love?
I ran from world to what's above;
Why hast thou come to me, a hermit,
When thy ways does my path not permit?
And why to thee feel I so near
When thy path from mine does far steer?

Thus spake Guru Gobind:
O Banda, my beloved ally,
I can give but one reply:
Know you not you came to wait
At this place so we could debate?
You came here to meet me alone,
For in your heart were my words sown
In lifetimes you cannot remember.
They glow within like silent ember,
Awaiting me to breathe your name
And stoke them into vibrant flame.

O Banda! How have you forgot?
Can it be you know me not?
There is no spot, no time or space
Where we dwelt not in the same place.
You serve me with your every breath,
And I'm with you in life and death.
No force can break our unique bond.
Your heart to me will e'er respond.
I scanned the earth to find just you,
And you were drawn, though no one knew,
To this place where we two could find
Ourselves and events, both in kind,
Were ripe for our auspicious meeting,
To set a course that's far from fleeting.

Thus said Banda:
O Guru, it no doubt is true:
I knew someone would see me through.
My heart was sure, though mind was not,
Someone would free me from this lot,
Someone to whom my heart would bow.
But if thou wouldst, please tell me how
I can be sure that it is thee
Through whom I should be ever free.
Could this be that momentous moment
When I'm released from bitter foment?

Thus spake Guru Gobind:
Why do these thoughts your mind give room?
I am your own. Let no doubts loom
To obscure our shared timely quest,
For you must rally to me, lest
The dharma fall into the dust.
Your service to me is a must!
I have awaited and have sought,
And held fast to the one bright thought
That you would come to help me when

The need arose, and until then
You would prepare yourself to offer
Your heart, your skill—all you could proffer.
You are my puzzle's missing part;
You are my own—my very heart!
Now put aside escape through doubting—
Give all such thoughts a sincere routing!

Thus said Banda:
O my Guru, I am sure
That brow so high and heart so pure
Could ne'er deceive nor lead astray;
But dare I here and now convey
To thee my life, for what it's worth?
I'm not sure why I took this birth.
O Guru, thou dost know me well.
I'm hoping thou wilt deign to tell
Me what my life is meant to be;
What purpose has't, I cannot see.
Please, Sir—clarify my mind.
Erase all errors thou wouldst find,
And purpose give this wand'ring searcher.
Please guide me; thou alone can nurture
This ragged, lonely, thirsty creature,
For thou art my belovéd teacher.
My mind with scripture's overflowing,
My frame from practice ever-glowing.
My own equation still eludes me,
And my philosophy deludes me.
It's over now, the life I've led.
It brought me here and now is dead.
I'm burning to know what is next,
Though try I might, my mind is vexed.

Thus spake Guru Gobind:
I shall convince you b'yond all doubt

So you will understand about
Yourself, your path, and your high calling.
Then you can progress without falling.
It's good to be clear at the start
So the base will not fall apart
Later, when it must be strong
To give support and prevent wrong.
So now I gladly give attention
To all your queries as prevention
For problems that might later rise
If s'lutions you can't now surmise.
For what occurs 'tween us today
At hermit's hut will hold great sway
For history and for our nation,
And for all those who seek salvation.
Just listen: I'll to you impart
That teaching I've held in my heart
Until I could to your ears give it
So you could come to know and live it.

Thus said Banda:
Oh, guide me now, for I am lost,
And by life have I long been tossed—
First to horror in the world;
Then in hermit's cave I curled.
Of pain I have found no surcease;
From sorrow there seems no release:
Though I am what men call advanced,
'Pon that solution I've not chanced.
Though I have searched inside and out,
My mind cannot the riddle rout.

Thus spake Guru Gobind:
O Banda, that indeed's the reason
I've come into this desperate season:
To bring you to the central point

So I can then your brow anoint
With wisdom of the middle path
By which you won't disturb the wrath
Of life by going off too far
To force a change or chase a star.
It is the path of skill in action
That brings the spirit satisfaction!

Thus said Banda:
But I have left the ways of strife,
Of making gain and taking life.
I've come too far to still pretend
That I could love the world again.

Thus spake Guru Gobind:
Do not misinterpret me;
You have my point yet to see.
Born were you for a life of service;
Don't let its burden make you nervous.
There is a way that you can learn
To carry it and let it burn
Your karmic seeds so it can be
Not barrier but means that free
You from your mind's painful delusion,
So you can dispel all illusion.
Adharma's fires rage blazing wild;
'Tis you must make those fires mild.

Thus said Banda:
I trust thy sense, but do not see
How I could solve this mystery.
Were I to go near evil's blaze
How could that my awareness raise?
Withdrew I to this lonely place
So I could realize God's grace.
The world cares not for such pursuits,
And I don't care for its cruel brutes.

4

The Middle Path

Thus spake Guru Gobind:
Beloved one, thy heart is troubled;
Your attitude the problem's doubled.
Leave off all of this backward thought,
And know you that the Truth you sought
Is even in those brutes you claim
Are vile. And lo, 'tis you who shame
The philos'phy of our greatest sages,
Who taught right action through the ages.

Now tell me where the world would be
If *sannyas** alone gave liberty.
The whole world is destruction wooing
If sincere seekers start pursuing
The path to which you now adhere.
It's not from love; it comes from fear.

If monks alone can reach the goal,
Then do you damn a mother's soul
For loving God within her spouse
And bringing child into their house
So she can serve it without stopping,
Forgetting self and never dropping

Her dear responsibility?
Her awesome capability
For selfless service, pure devotion,
Puts to final rest the notion
That monks are more advanced than she.
She too attains to liberty.
And what of him who works and prays
So she and children thrive always?
Is he who acts with skill and love
Denied the blessings from above?

Why is it we are all imbued
With penchant for romantic mood?
Is it some cruel celestial joke
To keep us captive in lust's yoke?
Or is it one more way that we
Can realize divinity?
The spark that lovers so admire
In their belov'd is God's own fire.
There is no other source for love:
It all comes pouring from above.

And why does man want to create?
That strong drive seems to be innate.
Is it just to inflate his pride,
Or does it come from deep inside—
This urge to bring forth something good,
Some thing that with right effort could
Reflect the glory of the One,
From whom all life's creations come?
Civilization as a whole
Reminds us of our higher soul,
And men have built it from within
As grace notes heard above the din.

You turned from these most lofty roles
And hid you under forest's knolls.

Were you so shocked to find it true
That nature has a dark side too?
Did you think life should not contain
The awful, ugly, bad—the pain?
You were a warrior; man, awaken!
'Tis sentiment has your life shaken,
And not some spiritual bolt
That led you to this stark revolt.
You've wandered unsure on your legs,
And now for balance your soul begs.

Now notice: you're not like these others,
These monks whom you have called your brothers.
They sit upon the village fringe
And on its people's milk do binge.
Or they enjoy their escape,
And stare off into space, agape.
But you came here to solve your query—
And aren't you becoming weary
Of staying here beyond your time,
Of rotting here while in your prime?
You've completed why you came:
Your yogic prowess warrants fame.
You do, no doubt, in yoga lead,
But I must ask you: What's the need
Of someone who knows the Above
But will not share it with his love?

The people are not being taught—
This is the battle to be fought.
You're right that they are not refined;
But will you plant it in your mind
That you may be a reason why
They are ignorant and shy?
You take the food from their hard labor
But will not do them the kind favor

Of serving them as they do you.
I thought that you already knew.
Are you much better than the wealthy
Who keep themselves happy and healthy
At the expense of the servile
Who have been trained to keep docile,
And thus assure their lowly fate
While those who crush them deny hate?
Oh, this heartless disparity
Is sadly not a rarity.
For though you have all caste foresworn
Yet cling you still to your forlorn
And harmful notion that your role
Is better than that of the soul
Who mates and labors in the world.
Your biased colors are unfurled.

The people's pain is in part due
To the outlook of men like you,
Who think a life of God requires
That they stoke only their own fires.
I pity their immunity
To knowledge of our unity.
From love I'm telling you all this.
I want you to enjoy pure bliss.

Thus said Banda:
I cringe in painful recognition
That thou portrayest my condition.
But one thing I don't understand:
Thy writings seem to countermand
The arguments you're giving now,
For thou hadst taken hermit's vow.
Thy writings do not give monks praises,
But it is found in several phrases—
Thou went toward what thou tell'st me leave.

Thou wert much higher—thou didst achieve
The rank of *rishi**, seer, and sage
In some lifetime before this age.

Thus spake Guru Gobind:
O Banda, do open your mind and your heart!
These concepts have been with us right from the start.
Aside put your intellect's sophistication,
And listen to me with complete dedication.
Our Sikh literature is resplendent and glorious,
Designed to inspire and make us victorious.
My own humble efforts, I hope, do the same,
As well as my innermost feelings proclaim.
My past lives prepared me for what I do now;
Though I'm a leader, inner life I avow
As the basis from which all good actions do flow
And the fountain from which inner quiet does glow.
Having lived as a recluse, you do understand
The deep-seated peace such a life can command.
In my days as a hermit, I contentedly strode
The valleys and glaciers of Himkund's abode.
My heart with devotion to God always sang,
My spirit soared freely; its ecstasy rang!
There I imbibed the profoundest awareness
And dwelt within constant refinement and rareness.
'Twas during that life the foundation was laid
For this lifetime's mission. Then also was made
The inner commitment that I would return
To instruct humanity so it could learn
That wisdom and action enhance one another
And that ev'ry person is like your own brother.
Can you have thought that I would conceal
A truth my heart told me to reveal?
Why remain silent on a topic so dear
To my heart as life as a recluse and seer?

You too have enjoyed the sweet solitude
That precedes your service to the multitude.

We have always believed that reincarnation
Goes on as a cycle of purification—
Each lifetime refining the lifetime before
And setting the scene for the next, to grow more.
We do not think this to be a superstition
But a relevant fact of the human condition.
When I was a rishi in deep meditation
The presence of God brought my soul elevation.
The Formless and Timeless I ever felt;
In oneness with God then I ever dwelt.
It was thus of my mission that I was informed,
And from then my actions as worship performed.

Thus said Banda:
Then life in seclusion can help one prepare
To help humankind its problems repair.
What thou now sayest doth ring true,
But some things I must still eschew.
Thou knowest it as well as I,
That life is transient, then we die.
The pleasures of the worldly life
Just magnify our inner strife.
Partners, jobs, and sensory pleasures
Distract us from our prime endeavors.
For we came here for one thing only,
And it's for that that we are lonely,
And not these fleeting gross illusions
That keep us blinded by delusions.
So if a man can pierce the veil,
Should he allow humanity's wail
To hold him from eternal bliss?
I ask thee—please explain all this.

Thus spake Guru Gobind:
You seem to wander to extremes;
Your arguments go on for reams.
I will tell you of your error
So you can be a wisdom-bearer.
From one perspective life's unreal
And from that view has no appeal.
But from a second, life's composed
Of those brief days that are enclosed
Between the cradle and the pyre—
So we should oblige all desire
While we still have the time and chance,
For life is just a fleeting dance.
There is a third view you can choose
If misery you want to lose.
And that is that the one real Source
Dwells within all, in all its force.
The Spirit cannot separate
From that which it does penetrate.
So finding out the one true Source
Can yet be done within the course
Of carrying out one's daily duty,
While working hard and loving beauty.
This is the way that I profess,
And those who follow it I bless.
So be a hermit in your heart,
But in the world take active part.
Let the ashes of service 'pon your body be smeared;
Let desires for goods be the locks that you've sheared.
Let chasteness of heart be the way you abstain,
And from escape to your hut let you ever refrain.

5

The Call of Dharma

Thus said Banda:
I understand thy point of view,
For its the one that I hold too:
I know the Source pervades the form,
And that is why my head is shorn.
I took up the monastic way
So I could live from day to day
In full awareness of the One
That is in all, excluding none.
This life has brought me to the heights
Far distant from the useless fights
That those devoid of wisdom wage
From narrow-minded selfish rage.
Whatever argument you pose
Could never make me one of those
Who complicate their days, and drift
Into life's whirlpool so bereft
Of purpose and of peace they think
That they must struggle lest they sink.
They have no sense of divine plan
And think of just one short life span.

I don't know why I should depart
From this path, which is full of heart,

And lose my lofty hard-won view
In effort to effect rescue
Of those who don't perceive their plight
And infect others with their blight.
I help the people from afar—
I needn't go to their bazaar
To pray for their waking,
For that would be mistaking
My role as holy man and guide
Who leads the people from inside.
I can do more from this thatched hut
Than can be done from that sad rut
In which the world creates its pain—
I'll help them from a higher plane.
Those few who really are sincere
Will find their ways to me right here.

Thus spake Guru Gobind:
My Banda, do beware of pride,
Lest in wrong thinking you reside.
It's easy 'mong the forest's trees
To disregard the human pleas
For wise men to become involved
So worldly problems can be solved.
It's easy in the mountain's heights
To forget all the human plights.
Abandoning your rightful action
Will never bring true satisfaction.
It's easy to renounce and claim
That others are the ones to blame
For all the suffering we see
When we look at humanity.
Renunciates do now abound—
No karma yogis have I found.
Worshippers of God, there're many—
Divine lovers, hardly any.

Half the seekers run away:
The other half remain and pray
To their own God in their own style
Insisting theirs is better, while
The others, sure theirs is the best,
Look with hatred on the rest.
You know there is but One in all,
Yet even you do build a wall.
What hope is there for those who feel
There's only one way to the Real?
The heritage of ancient sages
Taught tolerance throughout the ages,
But now the people fail to see
That love's the base for unity.
Despite their noble rich background,
No rest from suff'ring have they found.
And their society's decay
Is proof that they have lost the way.
What is the cause of all this pain?
It's because dharma's ceased to reign.
So pray you might to help them now
And cling fast to your hermit's vow,
But when values disintegrate,
Will you attribute it to fate?

This is a desperate vital hour,
When we must use all in our power
To keep the world from full decline
And rescue all that is sublime.
Yes, prayer is helpful, there's no doubt,
But direct action has the clout
That's needed now to stem the tide
And return honor to Truth's side.
Your world is made of ideal dreams.
Why do you go to such extremes?

You trod a different path before—
Why not resume it and restore
The dharma to its rightful place
And benefit the human race?
Be in the world and yet above;
Be on the path of work and love!
Why not become a rare example
Of all the grace that men can sample
By living holy, useful lives
Of service, through which one revives
The people's inner love of Light
And their commitment to what's right?

What good is it to just survive
If dharma can't be made to thrive?
You've found a tiny spot of peace,
But know you it must surely cease
When evil finds its own way here,
And you must lose what you hold dear.
By then the whole world will be lost,
And you must pay the final cost.
But you can prevent the whole fall
If you will now but heed my call.
The masses must learn to unite
And against evil soundly fight.
The tranquil, which you love so well,
Will listen to its own death knell
If you do not defend its life
And free it from impinging strife.
The balance is upset and skewed;
It will fall if it's not renewed.
The people must be ably led
Or hope for Truth is surely dead.
It's not enough to offer prayer;
For action's needed to repair
The loss of equanimity

Unloosed upon humanity.
The people must be led to live
As one and to Truth happily give.

The seeds that we sow make the fruits that we reap.
Our choice is clear: success or defeat.
Our actions determine the fate that we'll live
When present to future its power does give.
If devotion is not expressed in good deeds,
It cannot lessen humanity's needs.
Action devoid of love's divine touch
Can delay man's progress and harm it much.
Mankind has long suffered from this single cause:
Those who have power know not divine laws,
And those who do know them don't get involved.
Sri Nanak is great, for the riddle he solved:
Let men of the Lord not retreat from the world.
Let their wisdom and grace 'pon its fate be unfurled.
They have the love and the vision to guide.
Their values and motives make them qualified
To lead human destiny to its fruition
So it can move on from its sterile condition.
When people of God one by one can decide
To give to the world, then their love will preside.
The glory of dharma will then brightly shine,
Resplendent and patterned in its true design.
When dharma according to its form is aligned,
Then the progress of man can become more refined,
And the spiritual realm will inform every soul
So each person becomes more aware of the whole.

6

Dharma and Adharma

Thus said Banda:
Thou speak'st of dharma, and I know
In thy life does it clearly show,
But I think I pursue it too,
And yet we share a different view:
It led me here to dive within,
And it led thee to battle's din.
We're both sincere and true to heart.
How could we take a different part?

Thus spake Guru Gobind:
The difference is: my way chose me,
While you forced yours to your way be.
You are not being true to dharma—
You're just responding to old karma.

Thus said Banda:
I am amazed to hear thy speech,
For I thought dharma I did reach.
How could I be thus so confused
That dharma's ways I have misused?
The call I heard led me to here,
And to it my heart's ever dear.

If that was not my dharma's call,
Then I don't hear that call at all.

Thus spake Guru Gobind:
Of course you do, but it is quiet,
For you've decided to deny it.
It fell then silent inside you
And dwells beneath your conscious view.
But deeply there within your heart
Is dharma's cry: "Come, do your part!"

Thus said Banda:
Due to my mind I've not heard clearly
What my heart's guide told me sincerely.
I'm at last beginning to see fully now
How abruptly I chose to take hermit's vow.
I let my emotion rule over my mind
And followed a path of an unhelpful kind
For my unique nature and purpose in living,
Which is based on skilled action and selfless giving.
Now please help me to know what true dharma means
In case my mind dharma's view contravenes.

Thus spake Guru Gobind:
Dharma is the very fabric of being:
It sustains everything that you are seeing,
And upholds what you cannot see
From now unto eternity.
The dharma binds up all the loose pieces:
Under its harmony disruption ceases.
Dharma's the network that holds all the cells
That in the drama of life it propels.
If life on this plane has order at all
It's because good men have heeded its call.
The very word "dharma" expresses its goal:
To realize the unity of every soul.

Dharma's unchanging, and it's eternal.
Its precepts are loving and universal.
Dharma's the one underlying just code
That people of all nations see as hallowed.
If one takes away all the customs and norms,
Removes all the dogmas and social forms,
The single remainder that's left as the basis
Is dharma—the whole world's most sacred oasis.
Whatever supports life and spiritual awareness,
Whatever maintains growth and human fairness,
Is dharma. It's honor and goodness and love;
Its noble virtues emanate from above.
It has no confusion, no worry, no wrong;
Its perennial message remains ever strong.
In every era and in every time
It shows men the way to splendor sublime.
Virtues and values and higher endeavor
All come from dharma and emanate ever.

Non-harming, non-stealing, non-coveting goods;
Not misusing the senses nor telling falsehoods;
Purity, contentment, strong zeal for growth;
Self-study, surrender—these make up the oath
Of eternal dharma that applies to all
And gives them balance so they can stand tall.
There is nothing rigid or narrow or hateful
In dharma, for which all good men are grateful.
The sense of union and project and caring
Is dharma's; it leads men to enjoy sharing.
What makes people human and wholly mature
Is dharma, which did and will ever endure.
If some sense of bias or envy creep in,
Then it's not dharma—it's some kind of sin.
The ethics and morals of the eternal law
Are guidelines, not rulings to condemn a flaw.

Selfless is dharma; it thinks of the whole:
Serving the people is its sacred role.

Greed, pride, and ego are not in its scope.
Its lofty ideals give all people hope
That they can recover that great era when
Dharma reigned primal—they want it again.
For once was a time when the lives of all
Did under the influ'nce of dharma fall.
There were no armies, no courts, and no guards.
Each man was noble—of them sung the bards.
There was no need for society's rules,
For people loved goodness: they were dharma's tools.
Each person upheld the one sacred code,
And that made it easy to carry the load
Of human endeavor and human plights.
They didn't waste time in pointless fights.
So wisdom and service were the main pursuits;
They loved one another and had no disputes.
Their effort and skill went to their lofty goal:
The growth and upliftment of each human soul.
The spiritual purpose was their primal need;
They sought to fulfill it in every deed.

That holy time can be revived even now,
And that is the goal to which I avow.
It's within our reach to create it again.
It's a possible goal, and the highest of men.
All the great scriptures and prophets proclaim it;
All the great teachings in essence sustain it.
If every person to dharma would hold,
Man's ultimate destiny then could unfold.
The problems of mankind are due to rejection
Of dharma's precepts. We're under subjection
To thoughtless and selfish actions that kill
Not only the body but heart, mind, and will.

Once, leaders strove to bring dharma alive
And its light in the people's expression revive.
But conceit, lust for power, and competitive force
Keep leaders from tapping the dharma's true source.
Prejudice and pride keep the people apart.
They look to the difference, and not to the heart.
Self-centered, not selfless, they misuse their powers;
Then their human dignity in them but cowers.
By striving for power for only themselves
Into the mire of pain their soul delves.

But the great ones of history showed us the way
To live by the dharma even today.
No limiting outlooks distorted their teaching.
Its import is valid, correct, and far-reaching.
Though customs and dogmas might keep it hidden,
The sages revive it, for to it we're bidden.
The dharma is ours; it's our noble source.
We've but to accept it and follow its course.
It can't be imposed, but comes from one's heart—
It's been living there from the very start.
Dharma's the Truth, self-existent and pure.
But in midst of ignorance, it can endure
Only if people who love it do live it
And through loving actions to others regive it.

All the great illumined souls taught
That dharma is the goal to be sought.
The form that it comes in misleads not the wise,
They see beyond surface and always advise
Others to look past the trappings and see
That we are all one—we one family be.
Religion and nation create boundaries that seem
To highlight our differences to the extreme.
But the law of dharma is the law of love,
And we're all one people within the Above.

Dharma's eternal and helpful to all.
Without it, all meaning in life would then fall.
The most lofty ideals and precepts of man
Start inside with dharma, and then they expand.
Dharma's renewal begins in the heart—
And then in the world a man does his part.
Dharma extends beyond sect, caste, and creed.
It's boundless in spirit, and loving in deed.
Inner awareness shows dharma is true.
Then with it can man the whole world imbue.
By following dharma we attain complete bliss.
The wise know and practice the fullness of this.

The heartbeat and all that we sow
To dharma their existence owe.
The man of spirit its pattern sees
And through his actions its message frees,
To serve mankind in word and deed
And to fulfill the nation's need
To live in peace and have a glance
Of human wonder, divine dance.
The dharma embraces in every measure
Each one's tiny and profound treasure,
And finds in each one's tragic story
The seed that could release his glory
And free us from the human sorrow
That blights our hopes that come tomorrow
We can all as one family dwell,
And to one God our voices swell
In grateful praise and selfless giving
That we in love and grace are living.

Your high awareness makes you able
To keep the dharma sound and stable.
The dharma is in danger now;
We must uphold it—that's my vow.

So rally to this heartfelt plea:
Go now and fight the tyranny;
Go now and serve humanity
So that each person can be free!

7

Misuse of Ahimsa

Thus said Banda:
I want to serve humanity
Till every striving heart is free,
But I've embraced the ways of peace,
And for thee battles never cease.
I know what killing's all about—
That it is wrong I have no doubt.
I cannot do such heinous acts—
At the mere thought my heart contracts.
Could I inflict pain on a being
Because my view he is not seeing?
If I the Moguls were to slay,
I'd be barbaric, as are they.
Two wrongs do not make a right.
I speak from love and not from fright.
Ahimsa is a vow I've kept;
I hold it as my main precept.
Wouldst thou now want me to betray
My values? Do this doubt allay.

Thus spake Guru Gobind:
State you well non-fighting's view—
How I wish that it were true.

It is not clear to you right now,
But I've too kept ahimsa's vow,
And yet I've dispatched to the Lord
Ten thousand men beneath my sword.

Thus said Banda:
O my Lord, I am aghast!
Such horror is in sharp contrast
To the lessons thou dost teach,
Which tell man how to God to reach.
How canst thou in the name of God
Slay beings who were born and trod
In this same land as do we all—
Men who felt the same rainfall,
Who ate the crops and breathed the air,
Whose wives and mothers for them care?
And if I follow in thy lead,
Should I perform the same vile deed?

Thus spake Guru Gobind:
Do not be alarmed, my son.
Your gentle heart won't be undone
By taking up the life I lead,
For it to God does go with speed.
There is no contradiction here.
Our hearts are pure, and we hold dear
The gentler aspects of our life;
We do not look for useless strife.

Thus said Banda:
But we are all part of the whole,
And each man has a sacred soul.
The foot does not cut off its toe,
So how can one man kill his foe?
In doing that it's his own person
The life of which he does then worsen.

For we cells of one body be;
If I hurt someone, that hurts me.

Thus spake Guru Gobind:
You are right, in your own way,
But deeper, greater truths do lay.
For if a part be sore diseased,
The patient would be surely pleased
If the surgeon used a knife
To cut it out and save his life.
I am the surgeon for this nation,
And the sacred obligation
That I perform for its survival
Is cutting away any rival
To its spiritual welfare.
I have to, for we do not dare
Ignore a symptom that would grow
And create limitless great woe.
At some point we must draw the line
To prevent the further decline
Of principles that are required
To keep a culture's soul inspired.
For what's the use to be alive
If what has meaning can't survive?

Thus said Banda:
Thou think'st my head's up in the sky,
Yet for opinions wouldst thou die!
Life's a precious holy trust;
Preserving it's a sacred must.

Thus spake Guru Gobind:
I revere life, just as you,
But I can look beyond it too.
Our life is not remembered by
Its length before we had to die,

But by the legacy we leave
And what we're able to achieve.
We all must die; we've come to go;
The point is, what did we sow?
Did we remain forever true
Unto our hearts, or did we skew
Our values out of lust or fear?
Did we stand by what we hold dear?
Integrity and love are worth
All you can gather in this birth.

Thus said Banda:
But why should we get so involved
In conflicts that cannot be solved?
It's best to simply relocate
Than stay where men are filled with hate.
Why stay where one has got to fight
Just to survive—man's basic right?

Thus spake Guru Gobind:
I know you b'lieve in such escape,
For live you here past hermit's gate.
But were all the good men to run,
There'd be no struggle to be won;
For all those who had stayed behind
Would unrestrained themselves then find
To unloose any evil plan
And shift the destiny of man.
What of the suffering innocents—
Can your heart be deaf to their laments?
If you would think of true compassion,
Your views would shift in a deep fashion.

Thus said Banda:
But compassion is the reason why
I will neither kill nor die

In bloody battle where men fight
Displaying hatred and their might.
I feel true sorrow for the child
Whose father died in warfare wild.
He would not a poor orphan be
If only did his father see
A way to carry on his life
By moving his home out of strife.

Thus spake Guru Gobind:
You confuse mere sentiment
For something of profound portent.
You'd save the part but lose the whole,
Without which the part has no role.
If you save the whole but lose the part,
The whole can create a fresh start.
The part is just the price you pay
So the whole within life can stay.
Head can live without the eye,
But with no head the eye will die.
By saving eye at cost of head
Both will certainly be dead.
Give up the eye, and head will heal.
This is practical, not ideal.

Thus said Banda:
I know the view from thy great height
Extends beyond my poor short sight.

Thus spake Guru Gobind:
Then let your consciousness expand,
And contemplate the point at hand.
True compassion goes beyond
That of which we are now fond.
When we are trying to decide
Which way ahimsa would us guide,

We think of what will not begrime
The most within a span of time.
If that means we must strike a blow
To prevent evil, which would grow—
Then we do it with full calm,
Knowing it serves as a balm.
One must die to save the many;
Otherwise, there won't be any.

Thus said Banda:
But do not the wise scriptures say
"Indifference toward the evil pay"?

Thus spake Guru Gobind:
Yes, we should indifferent stay
As we send evil on its way.
We never slay in passion's throes,
For then we'd be what we oppose.
Nor do we loathe what we must do,
For through it Truth do we pursue.
We simply carry out our mission
So dharma finds its own fruition.
We are the instruments of fate;
It is beyond mere fear or hate.

Thus said Banda:
How can we dare to interfere
With Providence, whose view is clear?
It knows how life should best unfold
Without by us its being told.

Thus spake Guru Gobind:
Such passive thinking's a distortion of Truth,
Yet many are taught it from their very youth.
Don't go toward complacency. Do understand:
That lax weakness does success countermand.

It leads to ruin and erodes self-respect;
It's an insidious form of passive neglect.
Its basis is fear and negative thinking,
And many seekers succumb to it, sinking
Down with excuses till they think they're too tired
To come up from the pit where their energy's mired.
They call it ahimsa and think they are holy,
But it's not that at all. It is something lowly
That undermines virtue and makes one compromise
His values until he cannot tell what is wise,
But just does what's easy, what won't make a fuss.
So he acts not at all, keeps silent, and thus
He watches as life's pillars fall down into rubble
And thinks he has nothing to do with such trouble.
But one who stands by as good's made impure
Is responsible, just as if he were the doer.
Just think of the pain that is incurred
When to action the good are not stirred.
If goodness lets itself be destroyed
Simply to keep from acting annoyed,
Then it's no longer good at all,
For it allowed itself to fall.

Should the loving mother not be expected
To stop harm to which her child is subjected?
If a slap or a shout would work even faster,
Should she not impose it to prevent disaster?
If she won't protect her innocent child,
It could fall victim to the foolish and wild.
No mother stands by as her child goes to destruction
Without giving it warning and loving instruction.
And whenever she has to, she decisively acts
To remove that which 'pon her child pain exacts.
I am no different: I do intercede
So the will of God can man's supersede.

Thus said Banda:
I see the point thou art making,
Yet, within, my heart is aching,
For I've heard many soldiers claim
That their wars are fought in God's name.
Does each side not think that their God,
Who's born upon their homeland's sod,
Has told them to the enemy kill,
That it's the wish of divine will?
So one god's at war with another,
Inspiring brother to kill brother.
The Moguls say God's on their side,
And thou say'st God is thine own guide.
How can it be that God's for both?
Who is to say which is His troth?

Thus spake Guru Gobind:
It's not a matter of which sect or which race;
The just do not need to defend their own case.
Their goodness shines through despite what is said,
While the guilt of the evil can be easily read.
One's actions belie what is hidden inside;
In time it is clear if a party has lied.
The unrighteous don't follow an honorable code;
Their motive is selfish, and with torment they goad.
They're full of ambition and puffed up with pride;
They lie, cheat, and steal, and in cruelty hide.
The righteous defend what must not be let go;
They seek not a conflict, shirk not from a foe.
They are warriors of chivalry, valor, and mercy;
Their aim is for peace, not for more controversy.
Sharpen your mind and you'll be able to see
Who the true righteous and unrighteous be.

Thus said Banda:
But even if the sides are clear,
It's still to war that both adhere.

Were it not for the holy wars,
Then peace could open its sweet doors.
Religious fanatics take license to fight
And claim it's their preordained eternal right.
In the name of the spiritual they go to riot,
Creating such upheaval and unholy disquiet
That no one could contemplate upon the Lord.
They talk of their God, but they live by their sword.
Add national fervor to this rough confusion,
And the whole world's divided in awful delusion.
Politics—religious or national in nature—
Divests holy men of their spiritual stature.
How canst thou involve thyself in such low pursuits?
As a sage, wouldst thou not think that viewpoint pollutes?
There has to be another answer
Than keeping up this vile war-cancer.

Thus spake Guru Gobind:
Your points are noble, and I do respect them.
As for fanatics: I firmly reject them!
I'm no politician; I don't hanker for power.
But I'm born to lead people, and this is the hour.
I cannot resign from my life on this plane;
My destiny's clear: I must stop their deep pain.
They don't know how to forgo such fights;
They don't know how to preserve their rights.
I didn't create this awful pollution—
But while I'm here I must find a solution.
What choice is there but to answer the call
And prevent humanity from taking the fall?

Thus said Banda:
But surely there's some other useful approach
So upon the good, evil would not encroach.
How long must this tragedy be reenacted?
How long will men to war be so attracted?

I must tell you in truth that from war I'm repulsed—
The death and the pain—I'm in horror convulsed!
Bodies are strewn all about without care:
Here's crushed a head, and the arm's over there.
Where is the honor and dignity, when
Men visit such carnage upon other men?
There are no victors when we stoop to such levels.
All are uncivilized; the lowest urge revels.
The blood-lust engorges a man as a savage;
He thinks of nothing except what to ravage.
This senseless drama has just got to stop!
If the wise do not guide, the whole world will drop.
For one incident inflames at least fifteen more,
And soon the whole planet is at the last door.

Thus spake Guru Gobind:
Now calm yourself, Banda, and compose your mind.
We've come to the reason that you really find
Battle so awful: it your tender heart wrenches
To think of the men hurt and dead in the trenches.
Your sweetness and pity move your eyes to tears
To think of your brothers impaled on their spears.
And your sensitive sentiment is deeply appalled
When the fate of the widow and orphan's recalled.
I know how you feel, but I must say to you,
You're constraining yourself in a limited view.
The focus you're taking is strictly material,
And it's pushed you to ricochet to the ethereal.
You've reacted so strongly 'gainst dying and pain
That toward its sweet opposite do you now strain.
You cannot escape the stark facts of life:
Part of it's bound up in pain, death, and strife.
It's so immature to react to that notion
With heartfelt displays of tortured emotion.
To fall prey and indulge thus is spiritu'lly wrong.
Remember your philos'phy; be inwardly strong!

Compassion should never make anyone weak;
Your distortion of love takes you from what you seek.
This softness does not flow from a concerned heart
But reveals a rift that could tear you apart.
You're vulnerable, shaky, and have a thin skin.
Your mind harbors sentiment that is akin
To that of a young girl weeping o'er a hurt kitten!
How could a grown man be so strangely smitten?
Don't think me hardhearted or full of war zeal:
I just want you to look at the way that you feel.
Whom does it help if you're so overwrought
That you cannot take action due to a sad thought?
Your brooding betrays a strange morbid delight
In negative thoughts that do limit your sight.
Do you use this to explain
Why you from action do refrain?
If you're rendered useless by your revulsion,
Then you are the victim of a compulsion.
This recourse to the sweet and gentle view
Is limited, and it ill becomes you.
You oppose this struggle not because it's not right
But because the means is a gruesome and ugly sight.
Expand the spectrum of your feelings
So you can have some mature dealings.
Don't feign the holy by being susceptible
To pity and maudlin ideas detestable.
I know you're a brave man; I never doubted it.
But this sad emotion—you should have routed it.
Rally your awareness and fortify your strength!
Extend your perception to a much farther length.

Listen, O Banda, the soul never dies!
The loss of the body its power defies.
It lives on beyond the restraints of time
And dwells ever in the domain sublime.
No fear of death can disturb the aware

In the bliss of the spirit beyond compare.
Dying is nothing, and pains quickly fade.
They're often the price that has to be paid
To wrest from the darkness the forces of light,
Which we have to do with all of our might.
What other way to respond can there be
When the evil attack in a killing spree?
We're long past the point of adjustment or truce.
Nice talk to the death-bent is not any use.
They chose the means and the conflict, not we:
We just wanted peace so our souls could be free.
But now that they've snatched up our lives and our rights,
How can we just run from their unholy fights?
Without moral strength nations degenerate,
And the people have nothing to then venerate.
So channel your tendency to be so emotional
To dynamic expression of your devotional
Nature in service of the people's just need.
Act to defend them; they need you to lead!
Once you know firmly the issue is just,
Then upholding its life is an absolute must!

8

Collective Transformation

Thus said Banda:
Thy divine insight strikes me right to the core;
Thou needst not convince me of any more.
At last I see that true non-harming
May call for action that looks alarming.
I have been hiding in the life ideal:
It's time that I turned back to the real
And helped human problems with action and force,
Strongly defending the dharma's true course.
But how can I help humanity rise?
Can a few people the world spiritualize?
It seems when the masses in force act,
They lose their senses: is that not fact?
They lose sight of all wrong or right;
They care for only who has might.
And even if the cause is just,
They're overcome by greed and lust
For power, fame, or worldly pleasure
That they desire in boundless measure.
And even those who seem sincere
In time are swept into the sphere
Of selfish and unspiritual action
That crushes all in vile contraction,

While they still talk of holy mission.
They do not see the sad condition
Of those that they do claim to serve.
Caught in the whirl of collective verve,
They lose sight of the Truth within.
Then goal there is no hope to win.
I don't believe in collective change;
For error there's too broad a range.
Each person must his own way find
His web of karma to unbind.

Thus spake Guru Gobind:
The destiny of a family or nation
Is a larger design of one situation:
Each one's decision to accept Truth or not
Affects the entire universal plot.
As each person goes over to one side of the scale,
He adds there his weight, hoping his side will prevail.
As the votes are compiled, a majority forms,
And this designates the societal norms.
At some point, critical mass is attained,
And then are shifts in awareness sustained.
So change of the whole begins with each person
Who simply decides that he will not worsen
The plight of his friend, family, nation, or world,
But increases his love so with all it is swirled.
He heeds dharma's call in his own life first,
And when he is strong, other's needs are then nursed.
He determines to purify his senses and mind
So he can be useful, wise, loving, and kind.
Then he's an example and can show the way.
This is the man we're in need of today—
One who's controlled, who to dharma is true.
One who's aware sees the divine view.
If each one would only reform his own heart,
Then others would also soon do their part,

In time the whole nation would all do the same,
So freedom and justice could then ever reign.

Thus said Banda:
Sri Gobind, thou art indeed aptly named,
For the senses and mind hast thou wisely tamed.
'Tis thou who dost herd right the people's behavior.
Thou dost protect and guide them as a savior.
Thy radiance showest them the true source of delight.
And by thy glow does dharma come into their sight.
Sri Gobind, thou art the kind master of earth,
Destined to lead men from thy very birth.
By thee do men know the right way to live
So in divine service their talents they give.
Like Krishna the Cowherd, or Christ the Good Shepherd,
In thanks for thy guidance hath thy flock thee sceptered.
Thou hast taken my heart now into thy lead.
Thy message of love will I ever heed!
I want to awaken the people to change,
So progress can happen on a broader range.
Has such a change happened before in our history?
Will I ever be able to resolve the mystery?

Thus spake Guru Gobind:
You will inspire all to live by right action.
Their souls will expand—no more of contraction.
As each individual to your banner musters,
Polish their talents so each of them lusters,
And soon you will have a great radiant legion
Whose impact will carry throughout the whole region.
Change will then come in a broader way,
Leading humanity back in the sway.
Just as in the days of Rama,
When he set right the ways of dharma,
And peace was established across the land
So life could unfold as God had planned.

The story of Rama is inspiring indeed,
And provides all the lessons that you'll ever need.
Now look in more deeply to what I describe
So his valiant virtues you may thus imbibe.
Auspicious omens announced Rama's birth,
Preceding the avatar's life on the earth.
And although his youth revealed divine carriage,
He ascended his role only after his marriage.
For Sita, his wife, symbolized the oppressed,
And by her existence his whole life was blessed.
Her origin in life was indeed allegorical:
For the blood of slain sages is the metaphorical
Source that assumed her most beautiful form.
Evil King Ravana* and his wicked swarm
Tricked her and took her away from her home,
Compelling Rama to after her roam.
This unhappy event established the drama
Between the forces of dharma and adharma.
In face of injustice imposed by the cruel,
The minions who lived under Sri Rama's rule
But who dwelt as mere monkeys beyond the pale
Gathered their forces, swooped down like a gale
To rescue the queen of their majestic king,
Who was found by them because of her ring.
In harkening thus to the call of life's duty
They changed from within and revealed their true beauty.
That is the miracle that dharma can yield:
It transforms a person so strength he can wield.

Another example can be easily found:
For in Sri Nanak Dev such high virtues abound
As were glowing forth from the person of Rama
As he raised his people to the heights of dharma.
Guru Nanak Dev also upraised the nation,
Gathering its talents and uplifting its station.
They were dispersed and faint unto despair,

But he awakened their hearts and made them dare
To meet their potential and stop the oppressors
Without turning themselves into the aggressors.
He gathered many people into one single force
And in allegiance to God he followed the course
That allowed them at last to live in dignity,
To worship God and serve with benignity.
Avatars like Rama or Sri Nanak Dev
Thus rally the people, their spirits to save,
So each person can to his own self be true
And the whole can enjoy salvation too.

Just as one's spiritual progress requires
Sound mind and strong body as one aspires
To transcend the mundane and be not overwrought
By worries of survival or flesh, or be caught
By concerns of the physical of any kind,
Likewise it is true that for the world to find
Divine awareness it must assure the well-being
Of its physical too, with compassion freeing
The injustice and poverty that plague the earth.
Then to the spiritual can the world give rebirth.
This is the lesson Sri Guru Nanak Dev taught,
And for its acceptance he ever sought.
So all people in peace and harmony live
To be one with God and to selflessly give.
His program does thus not promote revolution,
But works to enhance spiritual evolution.

9

Sri Nanak Dev

Thus said Banda:
My Lord, when thou spoke thus of Sri Nanak Dev
Thou glow'st with a halo that radiance gave.
He was a savior who brought resurrection
To India's past of spiritu'l perfection.
And he did it, as dost thou, by skill in action,
Conveying that work is the soul's satisfaction.
The marvels he worked through the alchemy of Name
Transformed all his men—not one stayed the same.
Please tell me about that great mystic wonder—
That men could be changed, their blocks rent asunder.

Thus spake Guru Gobind:
You have, my disciple, brought up a principle
That explains why we Sikhs are so often invincible.
Sri Nanak Dev, God's instrument on earth,
Inspired his people to experience rebirth.
They had been living in defeat and despair;
For ideals and values they did not even care.
Their psyches were crushed and so was their culture,
Futility hung 'round their minds like a vulture.
Sri Nanak Dev's message fully inspired them.
He gave them dreams that zealously fired them.

Then they trusted in him, but more, in themselves.
He heartened their courage to go inward, where delves
The seeker of power, of wisdom, success.
And there they found God, who then did them bless.
They repeated God's Name with each breath of their life,
And thus they found valor and freedom from strife.
Sri Nanak Dev's love inspired them to create
Themselves and their world by the glorious template
Of dharma's great pattern of beauty and power.
It assured them success from that very hour.
He put them in tune with the way of the Lord
And kept them aloof from opinions untoward.
He focused them all on one single shared goal,
Chann'ling the Divine from within every soul
To uplift themselves and their people through love
So their every thought was directed above.
In this magic way—through God, goal, and prayer—
His people transformed, and now few can compare
With their dignity, reverence, and holy compassion
In service to God without any ration.

Thus said Banda:
O Guru Gobind, thou art the tenth in this line;
Tell me more of its founder, whose life does so shine
As a radiant model of human perfection
Worthy of homage and genuflection.

Thus spake Guru Gobind:
Your request makes me happy, for I'm always pleased
To remember our guru who our lot has eased.
Sri Guru Nanak is most surely unique
Among spiritual leaders of whom people speak.
He was neither a monarch nor the son of God,
But a gentle teacher who throughout the land trod,
Sharing his message with all who would hear it,
Living a life of compassion and spirit.

No auspicious omens did herald his birth;
He was a sage, not God on the earth.
He did not lead armies nor retire to the wood
But spoke from his heart and worked for the good.
He fed the hungry and helped the exploited,
Bestowed God's grace, and the people anointed.
Superior, yet simple, he was the people's friend—
Pathfinder, redeemer, their rights did defend.
Tyranny and oppression he would not abide:
He taught holy freedom, with God on his side.
He actually, in fact, professed little new,
But he brought ancient ideals into clear view.
He proclaimed the Vedas in living, practical terms;
Their intent in his discourses he reaffirms.
He revived the tradition so it proclaimed Truth
And not just the trappings that are learned in one's youth.
He balanced out the resurgence of evil,
Establishing order in the midst of upheaval.
The people rejoiced to find cure for their ill,
For he created an instrument of popular will
Through which their temporal and spiritual powers
Could join to assist them through difficult hours.
Sri Guru Nanak inspired them all
Till the soldiers of dharma answered the call
And created a kingdom of freedom and progress,
Where people could follow the dharma in oneness.

Sri Guru Nanak Dev was a spiritual man,
But he did not view this as placing a ban
On his active service in worldly affairs.
He offered his reverent, much needed prayers
Not just in words but in his constant effort
To instruct and inspire the people to exert
Their full potential together to build
A society designed to be as God willed.
His aroused social conscience impelled him to act

With a force of conviction that made great impact
On the quality and nature of life in his region
And the spiritual awareness of those in his legion.
The effects of his teachings resonate even now
After nine other gurus took up the vow
To help people live in spiritual dignity
And arise from the limits of social ignominy.
Hindus and Muslims alike did agree
That his was a mission that God did decree.
So they rallied together within his great cause
To uphold a life designed by holy laws.
They hailed him as guru, not because he proclaimed it
But because his demeanor and presence exclaimed it.

His tradition was not that of sadhu or priest
But of princes and generals whose lives increased
The quality of existence for the people they led.
To the people whose spirits and bodies were fed
By their noble efforts and shining example
They gave them on earth tastes of heaven to sample.
Men like Janak and Arjun who gave sacred food—
Kshatriyas, kings: men of great magnitude—
Were the ones who preceded him to the role
Of rousing the people, their hope to extol.
They built social perfection on a spiritual foundation
So all could be joyous in their great holy nation.
He taught not outer form but honored the essence
That pervades the form with its iridescence.
A man of the Lord, he knew that real worship
Means service to man and direct sponsorship
Of the dictates of dharma in their daily lives
So their essence unfolds and the network survives.
With spiritual motive expressed as humanitarian
He served to unite the nation Aryan.
His life portrayed that the one greatest prayer
Is to work selflessly for the human welfare.

Sri Nanak Dev was the first of his house,
All of whose teachers did rightly espouse
The wisdom of India found in Vedanta
And then simplified in the Sri Adi Grantha.
He embodied the teachings that he so adored
As he loved the people, whom he implored
To live by the noble ideas that were stored
In ancient scripture and the heart's own record.
For each human soul has the Veda within it
Needing only the guru or the word Infinite
To awaken that knowledge to the conscious realm
Where it can serve others with God at the helm.
The Grantha springs forth from the same lofty mountain
That upholds the Veda in its holy fountain.
The two as one flowed from Sri Nanak Dev,
The people of Punjab and the whole world to save.
He was the spirit of the Veda reborn,
The noble, high brow of Bharat to adorn.
His teachings came forth direct from the Source,
And he conveyed them with such a pure force
That his successors all had the strength to sustain
The high spiritual wisdom that he did attain.
They passed it on so our nation could grow
Along dharma's guidelines. Then it could show
Its ancient wisdom to the future ages,
So they could imbibe the Truth of the sages.
His inner teachings are told in the Grantha
So all men may come in touch with the pantha
That leads them to give to all and to share
Heavenly rapture and love b'yond compare.

10

Upholders of Dharma

Thus said Banda:
Thy words clarify and stir up my heart!
I am now prepared to do my own part
To keep Truth alive in the sphere of man,
To lift it upward again and again.
Though others forget and keep it all hidden,
I will remember and do as I'm bidden.
My life do I now completely indenture
To the speedy success of thy noble venture.
I offer my heart and my skills on the altar
That thou hast revealed. Now pray, lest I falter,
Temper thou further the steel decision,
And make thus impossible any recision,
By telling me more of the glorious deeds
Of saintly warriors upon noble steeds.

Thus spake Guru Gobind:
Now have you taken your rightful calling;
Guru will keep you from ever falling.
But listen, you whom my own heart holds dear,
As I make the nature of the warrior-saint clear.
From the time that Sri Nanak Dev told of his mission
His followers have gone through a profound transition:

Warriors do turn themselves verily to saints;
Saints become warriors with no meek restraints.
The two merge their qualities, lo, into one.
This is the path Nanak Dev had begun.
His way was one of pure, vibrant devotion,
With no rote constraints to dilute the emotion.
India before had burst forth bhakti's shower
But never in the way that it did in that hour.
Before, bhaktas* chanted in praise and humility,
Prostrating their minds, generating docility.
Their idealist doctrine and love for tranquility
Made action to them seem a wasteful futility.
Bhakti could be a haven for those who lacked
A practical outlook and the will to act.
But the Sikh bhaktas were a different breed.
They responded to love and to the need
To serve God by serving each human being.
When they looked at man, 'twas God they were seeing.
Their chorus unceasing the Holy Name sang,
Their hearts with increasing compassion then rang.
They mastered the ecstatic bliss of devotion
Perfected by bhaktas, and added the notion
Of service through skillful and valorous action
To enhance their absorption—it was no distraction.
They expressed not by swooning and shedding their tears
But by giving their service throughout all their years.

They differed on one more significant point:
By no forms of God did the people anoint
Their worship, but rather sang only the Name
Of the formless, eternal, and always the same.
For that song they needed no ritual or priest.
It rang in their hearts and gave sound to the feast
That daily they shared with all the community,
Casting off bias, enjoying their unity.
The One they acknowledge permeates all.

Thus 'pon a deity do they not call,
But muster their forces to defend their right
To follow the Truth—thus they have divine might.

The boundless energy this approach gave
Built up to be an immense tidal wave
That swept right across the Aryan nation
Rallying hearts to a social ovation.
Harnessed and channelled, it flowed with such fury
That all souls were drenched in its wondrous flurry.
In rushed its poetry, quick as a flood,
With image and metaphor stirring the blood.
By strength of its inspired and fervent rapture
The heart and the soul of the Sikhs did it capture,
And sent it, charged, reeling out to create
Their future—a destiny to radiate
All over the world, so it would permeate
The people with zeal and thus obviate
The need for disaster to open their eyes
To the truth they then would at last realize:
That if humanity is to survive,
It needs compassion to stay alive.

According to Nanak each man is a leader;
He shares that high peak with every acceder
To the throne of service from which all do reign.
The leader of leaders in this regal domain
Is the guru, of whom I will soon be last,
For the need for the post is a thing of the past.
The people, for longer than two hundred years,
Have well learned the teaching and are free of fears.
They will still follow the line of the ten,
But never will only one man guide again.
The lineage of gurus—from Nanak to me—
Will live in the Grantha and the Five's decree.
No individual should wield such a power,

For under its burden do mortal men cower.
The spirit of guru sat on only ten heads.
From now it will live in the light their word spreads.
The guru now will show the pantha
Within words of the Adi Grantha.
Not just one man will have the last word,
But from the Five will Truth then be heard.
With the Grantha and their wise decision,
My Sikhs can continue with precision
To complete our mission's holy work—
Which opposes neither mosque nor Turk
Nor any other path, clan, caste, or nation:
It fights for Truth's continuation.
Our way is love and affirmation,
Never bias and condemnation.

In my house we accepted all,
And lust for power did not enthrall.
We never sought out land or title.
We did not strike first—that was vital.
We always sought to reconcile
And forgave those who were hostile.
We sang first hymn, then battle cry
When others did our peace deny.
We stood then to protect the right.
'Twas not worldly; 'twas of the Light.
Our house holds concerned, holy men
Who upheld right with acumen.

The gurus were men of action and spirit both,
For the welfare of dharma in truth is their oath.
Many teachers have there been, both ascetic and stoic,
But few have there been both divine and heroic.
My ancestors, each one, were men of the Lord,
And many were versed in the skill of the sword.
Poets they were, of aesthetic refinement,

Yet adept in the ways of worldly consignment—
Like Drona, so learned in the use of arms;
Like Bhishma, rallying the troops to alarms;
Like Rama, benevolent and righteous as king;
Like Kabir, the praises of God e'er to sing.
They harnessed the power that's greatest of all:
Dharma—whose forces do ever enthrall.
The high gods of yore remained mere observers—
At best they sent forth their greatest preservers
To sustain the dharma by killing the foe—
But our gurus themselves carried arrow and bow
And used them in battle 'gainst devil and demon
To insure that people could then live in freedom.
Thus did the gurus create a new role:
They saved the nation and fulfilled the Goal.
Each one passed the banner on to the next.
And now it resides in our Holy Text.
For the work must continue; it must never be lost,
No matter what forces try Truth to accost.
The depth of their valor for justice is rare:
Just think of my father and that youthful pair—
My sons who happily gave up their lives
In the knowledge that justice and dharma survives.
My Five Beloveds gave their heads the same way
On that historic Baisaki Day
When the order of Khalsa was molded to guide
The next generations onto dharma's side.
They are foresworn to uphold the right—
Regardless of end or result of the fight.

Their bravery is based in spiritu'l sources.
Nothing can shake the impact of their forces.
With souls of steel and hearts ablaze
The enemy do they awe and amaze.
The foe's evil breast is filled with dread
As they aghast see the forces ahead,

Charging with swords and with sacred songs
To protect the Truth, for which man longs.
Just the mere sight of them makes their hearts quake
Sounds of their chants makes their very limbs shake.
There is no resistance that can ever succeed
When devotion and action to power accede.
These holy warriors serve the future of man.
When they unite, then the divine plan
Will prevail over any other possible power.
You must lead them, O Banda! This is your hour!

11

Truth or Tradition

Thus said Banda:
I will uphold the dharma's shield!
With all my might to thee I yield.
To do so I must lose this doubt
That I would now ask thee about.
How can I make the differentiation
If not by sect, creed, clan, race, or nation
'Tween those who love dharma and those who do not:
I want to be sure I protect whom I ought.

Thus spake Guru Gobind:
In every great life comes a moment of test.
Thus have I faced both the worst and the best.
The evil are those who would oppose justice;
The allies support it and show that they trust us.
Many the Muslims who fought by my side;
Right beside me some of them bravely died
Defending the Truth for all to enjoy
Regardless the worship that they employ.
My Muslim disciples saved me from great dangers,
While some of the Sikhs turned from me like strangers.
One's clan does not indicate if he is good,
But his heart and actions most certainly could.

One shouldn't expect external signs to portray
What only the depth of the heart can convey.
It has little to do with religious systems,
With external customs or with narrow dictums.
So learn to look into the heart of a man—
That tells you much more than appearances can.
We Sikhs base our judgements on virtue, not creed.
A truly good man shows his worth by his deed.
We gladly accept all, and we exclude none,
For after all, we're the same—we are one.

We're positive and practical in our approach;
'Pon cripplers of spirit we fiercely encroach.
We will not unwittingly stoop to become
The tools of adharma; we must have freedom
From prejudice or bias of any form.
Such narrow opinions we o'ercome by storm.
Our beloved ancestors laid down their lives
For noble ideals that each heart revives
By beating with deepest compassion for all,
Lack of which would be our fatal downfall.
We fight adharma wherever we see it,
Without or within, whichever be it.
It's not a mere person or group we oppose,
But demonic thoughts are our only real foes.
So we destroy them in our own minds too,
With just as much valor and derring-do
As we use to defeat the adharmic forces
That attack the dharma from external sources.
And we are happy to die, if we must.
At worst, our having to die is just
A passage to time when we again serve;
At best we into the timeless One merge.

Do not think our struggle a partisan one:
It is universal; there's no one we shun.

Even a foe is forgiven the minute
He accepts the dharma and the Infinite
By whatever name he chooses to call It.
We welcome their gesture and never forestall it.
Adharma and dharma are the only two
Differences that my warriors ever knew.
So if your eyes ever catch 'pon a difference in style,
Just look with your heart, see the One, and you'll smile.
If one follows adharma, wrong action will show it.
He can't hide his hate; you can't help but know it.

Thus said Banda:
Thy beneficent wisdom surpasses all others!
Thou dost truly embrace all people as brothers,
And reach to the essence that joins us all,
Whether to God we dance, march, or crawl.
Thy Sikhs do not uselessly waste their might
On any petty or partisan fight.
Their ancestors taught them to see One in all,
And only for dharma do they heed the call
Of recourse to battle, as a last endeavor
To prevent the Truth from fading forever.

Thus spake Guru Gobind:
The great Sikhs of yore were noble and grand.
When injustice prevailed, they took a stand,
And feared they not then for the body's survival
But only for freedom and dharma's revival.
They bowed to the joy of discipline's hand
And sought not for looting or conquering land.
They submitted to *tapas** but never adharma,
For they were committed to burning off karma.
They were warriors and saints steeped in the Lord,
Upholding the dharma with discriminate sword.
Their clarity of purpose and purity of heart
Guided their steps so they could not depart

From the path of God toward the way of man,
Which is strewn with allurements more powerful than
Most men can endure without losing sight
Of the just, holy motive requiring their fight.
They never struck out but as last recourse,
And when they did, they were one with the Source.
No malice or anger crept into their feeling
As duty compelled them into battle reeling.
They did not aggress nor plot to do harm,
But responded with skill to any alarm.
Then with sword in hand and with Name on lips
In calmness and strength they endured hardships.
If death was their fate, then death they embraced,
For their love of dharma its horror erased.
They fought not for petty, sectarian reasons,
But for purpose enduring through countless seasons.
Their lofty ideals, universal views,
Kept their hearts open. They would not abuse
The ways of their neighbor's custom or path.
They sought life in peace, eschewing vile wrath.

They knew the difference 'tween Truth and tradition:
One is eternal, the other addition
Developed by men to retain and enhance
A means to acquire their certain entrance
Into the realm of Truth. Truth alone warrants
That one stake his all to fend off the torrents
That assail and forestall its continued reign.
Traditions are temporal and worldly in vein,
For they come and go, being means and not end.
Many they are, and them time does amend.
Varied in structure, in content diverse,
They all, despite difference, are ways to traverse
The treacherous region that won't let one enter
Into the realm of Truth. Truth is the center
Toward which great traditions all lead without fail.

Truth is essential, but don't go through travail
And upset your progress through unruly fights
To preserve mere customs and mere social rites.

The right Guru Nanak Dev strove to defend
Was the right to seek Truth. He did not descend
To squabbles about ways one could reach the goal;
He just wanted freedom for each human soul.
We love our tradition; for Truth we would die.
Tradition will vary; Truth never deny.
The Truth remains one and the same—infinite.
Adhere to it steadfast through life's last minute.
And protect its expression here on the earth
In the moment of death, from the moment of birth.
That's the ideal Sikh dharma stands for;
For that right alone would we ever wage war.
If Truth is lost in attempt to protect it,
Then the effort is futile, and one should reject it.
It's better to seek Truth in a more subtle mode
Than cling to a style yet lose track of the road.
So follow the Truth with mind, action, and speech,
And the Absolute One you will certainly reach.

12

Beyond Duality

Thus said Banda:
I know the real miracles thou dost perform:
My own powers pale 'fore the way they transform
Bairagi to Banda by power of thy word;
I'm completely changed since thy teachings I've heard!
Thy blest, fiery speech now enraptures my ears.
I cling to thy feet, washing them with my tears.
Thou dost command well both the word and sword;
The Almighty Mother hath blest thee, my Lord!
And now thou dost choose me to perform thy task:
I'm thine to command—whate'er thou might ask.

Thus spake Guru Gobind:
Yes, you are called to complete what's undone.
But don't praise me so—I'm a tool of the One.
Each person his role must play out in his time—
The one difference is that I'm sure of mine.
What talents I have my guru did impart.
He told me, "Keep Goal, God, and Name in your heart."
I'm a simple man blest with divine love.
I'm like other men—I'm not up above.
I'm here to serve people, as you do too.
Don't place me above life—there's so much to do.

As you, I serve God—there is no difference there.
Our work must continue; please do not compare.

Thus said Banda:
My Lord, I know that we are one, and that is all there is,
But for the sake of joy and love, I point out differences.
My heart tells me there is just One, and that I do believe.
But eyes do see diversity, and boundaries I perceive.
Just as I see thee and me as two as well as one,
So see I another pair where there perhaps is none.
For fight thee now in dharma's cause, while others make it fall.
How can all this be happening when Truth exists in all?

Thus spake Guru Gobind:
You've found the wonder deep inside—
That Truth and fiction co-reside.
Fiction it is and Truth it is too.
Don't let this paradox overwhelm you.
Both Ravana and Rama live,
And to each other purpose give.
A single rod must have two ends,
And on the other each depends;
The same is true in daily life:
Enjoyment comes to balance strife.
If something comes, it surely goes—
And that is true of joys and woes.
When there's abuse, defenders rise,
And all the virtues they comprise
Are equal to the evil done.
Thus do they fight till one has won.
For every villain makes the need
For heroes his way to impede.
The two are always intertwined
And in their drama thus confined.
Just like two banks of one river:
They merge so life can flow hither.

Together they do form the groove
In which the stream of life can move.
One's existence needs the other;
If one ceases, ends his brother.
This is the way of world's reality:
It's bound up in pairs of duality.
But beyond that, in realms divine,
There's really nothing of the kind.
It takes a monumental shift
To just eradicate the rift
Between the pairs that is perceived
When life's duality's conceived.
For when one views life from the One,
Of opposites then are there none.
For then at last the poor mind dares
To see the rod and not the pairs.
Then he can know that two are one:
That Ravana and Rama are spun
Into one cloth, and that in truth
One is the warp, and one's the woof.
If one is taken from the weave,
The other too its place must leave.
So Ravana's the happy flaw
That does from heaven Rama draw,
So they may act their poignant drama
And poets sing the Ramayana.

Our role upon the field of action
Is to put limit to the fraction
Of energy bound in evil's sway.
You must now know it's nature's way
That evil grows strong on its own,
While seeds of goodness must be sown.
Thus, spirit cannot ever dally—
'Gainst evil must it always rally,
Lest blind and selfish interest reign

And humankind submit to pain.
So ignorance must be contained;
The way of Light must be proclaimed!
Some darkness there may always be,
But one must hold the torch to see.
The question is, then, who will reign:
Deluded people, or the sane?
The drama has this at its center:
If e'er the hero fails to enter,
There then will be no contest run
And by default evil has won.

Amid the vastness of black brine
A tiny spark of light does shine.
Its flickering must be ne'er lost;
We must defend it at all cost.
The real Truth is a sacred trust,
Preserving it an abs'lute must.
From this challenge there is no turning.
Denying it racks hearts with yearning
To return and fight till we drop
So the light might ne'er ever stop;
For die we will—that is for sure—
But will we then be vile or pure
Depends on how we waged the fight:
Defending darkness or the Light.
With this in mind, it is clear why
The dharma's guards do kill and die
Without a twinge of hesitation.
For each life is a grand oblation
That's offered to the sacred fire
To free us all from darkness' mire.
This action is performed by man
When evil could 'gainst goodness stand
So strongly that it hides the Light.
The worthy then have got to fight.

And woe to all if they will not—
And woe to those who chose the lot
Of fighting 'gainst them if they will.
For they relentlessly will kill
All those who dare to tip the scale
Upon the side of those who fail
To help them in that sacred hour
When they unleash their awful power,
And tear down all that robs the right
Of men to live in Truth and Light.

Thus said Banda:
Thou tellest well the task; yet I can see,
No surcease from it will there ever be.
On levels of phenomenal existence,
We must maintain with ongoing persistence
To keep the tide of evil at bay
And insure the righteous a clear way.
But do forgive this negative thought:
If in a downward gyre we're caught,
And even the godly must work to stay afloat,
Then chances for progress seem completely remote.
Is the same drama to go on forever?
Will one side or the other prevail never?
It seems an endless practice in futility;
I don't see that it has any utility.

Thus spake Guru Gobind:
Dense, dark discouragement pervades your view.
You're a holy man; it ill becomes you.
Evidence of the downward draw is ample
Without using yourself as an example.
How well do lofty principles conceal themselves from view
If with them through experience we don't ourselves imbue.
That's why all mystics who are Sikhs within the world stay active
And hold inner and outer views as equally attractive.

It's not a choice of living in the world or 'bove it;
But one must find the way to be in both and love it.
Look now, your question indicates that you forgot to see
The drama as an aspect of the one Reality.
Think you there is no way free from this unending toil?
Will the darkness ever all our hopes for more light foil?
From the view of dualism, the play goes on and on,
But from the view behind the screen, then it is gone anon.
When the world you can perceive while keeping view of both,
Then will you success attain in your next phase of growth.
Awaken you unto the fact that light in darkness dwells.
And when you can reside in light, you feel not darkness' spells.
Wise is he and rare the one who sees the light, yet stays
Amid the realm of those who dwell unknowing of its rays.
For them the drama never stops, no matter what their role,
But one who dwells within the light becomes one with the whole.
He sees the drama, sees its end, and sees it start again.
He sees the sets, the props, the stage, the actors' acumen.
He knows it is important now; he knows it matters not.
And so he gives his heart to man to help its desperate plot;
And so he keeps his heart within, content behind its locks.
This is the myst'ry of the sage; he is a paradox.
He gives his all and is not there;
He strives to win and does not care.
Who can understand this strange capacity?
Who can comprehend his vast sagacity?
Even the nearest disciple, O Banda, cannot penetrate
The marvelous folds of wondrous *maya** that ever radiate
About the guru's luminous field,
Protecting him just like a shield.
And thus the holy drama of depriver and deprived
Conceals the private hidden Source from which it is derived.
The drama goes on as it must, and players play it well,
But masters play it knowing that it is but maya's spell.
That rare knowledge serves them to intensify their skill,
Yet they've given all they are unto the divine will.

Victors rise and cultures fade;
Gods recede who once were paid
High praises vast. Noble lords
With glowing shields and gleaming swords
Are now forgot and turn to dust;
Their weapons and their honor rust.
O Banda, do you wonder why
We all are born if we must die?
Why must we daily take in food,
No matter if we're in the mood,
When by tomorrow hunger's growl
Will once more set us on the prowl?
And is it not a futile scene—
This constant battle to keep clean?
Just think of all the work and time
That's wasted warding off the grime
That migrates back to where we scrubbed
As soon as somewhere else we've rubbed.
You think I jest, but don't you see?
These are the questions you've asked me.
Of course, the ebb and flow go on,
And that's what life is based upon.
So we must ride well on the tide,
While knowing that from deep inside
It's shallow—yet we must still do it;
It is our duty to pursue it.
For thus we pierce through to the goal
And merge with universal soul.
Those who have thus seen the Source
Are drawn to help by dharma's force.
For if the balance ever wavers,
Dharma's power sends its saviors.

13

Beyond Psychic Powers

Thus said Banda:
Thou hast now revealed the truth so that I understand.
I am grateful to be here within thy great command.

Thus spake Guru Gobind:
My heart does sing and I am glad
That you acknowledge our dyad,
For it is one death ne'er can sever,
And aught can break it now or ever.
I'm happy you are here with me
And with this mission you agree.
But I want to see that you know
It is a holy path also.
You left the world, forsaking home,
And with wise sadhus did you roam,
But tell me, from the path you claim
Can one enlightened one you name?

Thus said Banda:
O Guru, thou dost my powers test
To tell the saint from all the rest,
For know thou that they love to hide
And keep their secret locked inside.

And any one who dares to say
That he's a sage does thus betray
The fact that he is surely not—
And one who that prestige has got
Would never lower himself by
Announcing that he is so high.
Some signs of progress, true, are known,
So we can tell how much we've grown,
And hallmarks of the sage are written
So by a fake we won't be smitten.
But if thou tell'st me to report
Of whom I've seen, I must retort
That in my life, though I've seen many
Wise adepts, I don't know any
Who have reached to the highest peak—
Except for thee, to whom I speak.

Thus spake Guru Gobind:
Not even one on that highest rung—
Where dwell seers, and wise unsung
Wonders of the yogic lore? And even you,
My Banda dear, I know high yogic feats can do.
Surely in this hermitage designed
For spirit, one soul has been consigned
To rapture of *samadhi's** height
And wrapped within the divine light.

Thus said Banda:
Oh, there are many who've attained
Such heights, and powers they have gained,
But these are only lower stages
Experienced by all of the sages.
They are just the final few steps
On the stairway of the adepts.
I know because I've climbed them too,
And they amaze the mind, it's true,

And fill the heart with blinding light,
And yield rare powers of great might.
I do not boast, but to explain,
These powers fall like the spring rain.
The *siddhas** enjoy remarkable skill:
They control nature by use of the will.
They walk on water, fly through air—
They do things others do not dare.
They stand unscathed amid the fire;
They can stay pure within the mire;
They shrink down smaller than an ant,
Or billow up like elephant.
They talk with spirits and move big rocks.
These are their powers; these are their blocks.
But these skills do not an enlightened man make;
And what meaning have they for humanity's sake?
For me, I know there must be more.
I've not yet reached the other shore.
I must dwell here far from the squalid
To keep my lofty powers solid.
I am the captive of my attainment.
I don't dislike that rare containment,
But dwelling at its lofty heights
Requires me to lose my sights
Of people and their sad condition,
Which isn't of my own volition.
I want to be like lotus flowers,
Who have it in their gentle powers
To dwell in earth yet stay above.
They stay in mud because of love,
Yet face upward unto the light:
Their posture seems exactly right.

Thus spake Guru Gobind:
I know you are a special being
And agree that you're rightly seeing

The lotus as the perfect image
As symbol for the yogic lineage.
You are a yogi who is widely renowned
For having mastered the science of sound
And for having countless remarkable powers
That the Divine graciously upon you showers.
You have to me listed the talents of wonder
By which you could cast aspersion asunder.
But that which is needed at this vital hour
Is no such display of supernal power.
Those powers are proof that you do comprehend
The way nature works, and that you can amend
Its course of events so people wax lyrical,
Astounded in awe to see such a miracle.
But the siddhi you need to hold like a chalice
Is control of your mind, and freedom from malice.
You should be the model of pure love in action;
Your followers and foes should be swept by attraction
To attend to your message and ascend to the karma
Of being a follower and upholder of dharma.
I want to teach you to love and to serve
So you can help others with selfless verve.
You've gone toward holy, meek, and mild,
And you've known outward, brave, and wild;
You've been both docile and demanding:
Of opposites you're understanding.
I have respect for your brave heart;
To you my wisdom I'll impart—
For my purpose as guru is to awaken
The talents and truths that you have forsaken.

14

The Essence of All Religions

Thus said Banda:
I want thee to awaken me.
Disciple I will ever be;
With thy words I do comply—
But there's one thing I can't deny:
I want to hear thee say direct
That thy path is for the elect.
I want the purest spiritual teaching,
Not the taste that's shown in preaching.
Please now convince me of its stature:
I'll follow it in grateful rapture.

Thus spake Guru Gobind:
You place me in a delicate bind,
For know you, paths of any kind
Are fine if they to God do lead;
It matters not which name they heed.
The path I love's universal in bearing;
For non-essentials, I have no caring.
Whate'er the mode one uses to start,
The path he keeps is one of the heart.
The variety of paths and creeds makes confusion
That only increases the people's delusion.

Each sect claiming it's truest and best
And putting itself above all the rest.
This nullifies their purpose for being.
Instead of the One, it's difference they're seeing.
The inherent truth that I always proclaim
Is that all paths to God are essentially same.
The variety we note on the surface is culture's,
Yet critics swoop down upon it like vultures,
Picking at pieces of a religion's body,
Condemning any aspect unique as shoddy—
As if the spirit of that faith could be affected
By the oddness or error in style they'd detected.

It matters not what the mode or the form
A religion may carry to comply to the norm
Of the era and culture in which it began.
And it matters not what the sect or the clan
One has when he's born—we all have the right
To follow the path that leads us to Light.
Whatever good story or trapping inspires us
Can be the first step in a path that requires us
To finally let go of all such non-essentials.
When we look to the core of a system's potentials,
We find hidden deep in its major teachings
Lessons more lofty and subtle than preachings.
There, beyond all of the surface conditions,
Past levels of rivalry, and superstitions,
Shines the one single core of spiritual verity
That is found by all seekers who look with sincerity
For the true inner meaning their faith does convey,
Despite any contrasts outer signs might portray.
When one reaches the heart of the path that he claims,
It is clear that no meaningful difference remains
Between his outlook and that of another
Whose method may differ from that of his brother.

There is only one purpose for the spiritual quest;
There is only one outcome: to be fully blest.

Why people want to fight over ritual
Has nothing to do with anything spiritual.
It is an unrighteous abomination
To think of a squabble as a laudation.
Could God or Reality really be pleased
By bickering minds with hatred diseased?
All paths I know of teach one thing for certain:
A negative mind that's upset draws a curtain
Heavily hanging 'tween the Divine and the person
Who with disturbed thoughts his condition does worsen.
The Divine can be known if the mind is composed,
But emotion-tossed minds are directly opposed
To the spiritual purposes of any seeker.
So it's clear that one's spiritual zeal becomes weaker
By allowing the mind to become so concerned
Over issues that from our mere customs are learned.
Our diverse ideas add texture to life;
They're not to be used to create any strife,
And especially not by those ones who seek Truth.
That they would do something so low and uncouth
Is ample to banish them from their attainment
And strip them of whatever spiritual raiment
They had up to then been able to acquire
By their sincere efforts and lofty desire.

Now back to the question you did previously pose:
Is my path superior—is it highest of those
By which men aspire to divinely progress?
With no shade of doubt, I can answer you—yes!
For the path that I follow is the one beyond time,
The essence of all, beyond era and clime.
It's the internal core of all paths that exist,
And its draw is so strong that no one can resist

But to search for it in every breath that he takes.
Even if the spiritual quest he forsakes,
He looks for its beauty in sensory delights;
He sees hints of its glory in success's heights.
The compelling charm glowing forth from the sage
Is proof that another can reach to that stage,
To that highest peak to which he ascends
And upon which each of his wonders depends.
My path is the real essence found in all others,
Its beauty their density frequently smothers.
Yet those who dive into the depths always find it;
However they start, they eventu'lly unwind it.

All the great sages have taught this same way,
But distortions of others made them seem to say
Something different, when spoken by their rigid preachers,
Whose dogma did not come from their spiritual teachers.
Religions are man-made and subject to errors,
But spiritual paths are taught by Truth-bearers.
All the Sikh gurus have taught this is true,
And the Bhagavad Gita supports it too.
The sayings of Jesus and Buddha and Sri Shankaracharya
Are expressed in the Koran, the Granth, and Kabala.
So don't start comparing and condemning the ways
That your brothers use to make sense of their days.
Rejoice they can find one to which they are suited,
And follow the one that in your heart is rooted.

Thus said Banda:
My heart loves the path that thou dost describe;
Its essence in all paths I need to imbibe.
I did not realize till it was told clearly
That the path I have cherished ever so dearly
Is the same one that thou hast just told me about,
And to it I will always be most devout.

The decision of whether to find satisfaction
In my hermitage or in the world of bold action
Resolves itself neatly, now that I've discovered
That these seeming differences have only hovered
Over the surface of the real one true way
Whose essence I am finally seeing today.
My days of career and retreat from the world
Prepared me to walk the route thou hast unfurled.
O my Guru, my heart rests at thy lotus feet.
Direct me to take up the course I must meet.

Thus spake Guru Gobind:
Since you know that your feet tread the path of light
And your inner eye has the clarity of sight
To discern that the One does this world sustain
And to see that the Spirit imbues the mundane,
You won't be deluded by the world of diversity
And risk being swayed by baseless perversity.
In your own life you have known the two poles
And the dire fate that extremism holds.
So I do trust you to remain ever loyal
And know that my mission you will never spoil.
So, I place in your hands the tremendous task
Of showing the people in one God they bask,
And help them to find some helpful solution
So they uphold the dharma, and not the delusion.

15

Transformation

Thus said Banda:
Thy precious words give my heart bliss.
Upon thy feet I'd place my kiss,
For I am sure you are my master.
I wish that I could progress faster,
But my mind holds still one thought yet,
And when it flees, then thou wilt get
Total surrender, me to thee.
Then what thou orderst, I will be.
I want to be completely sure
That on this path I can endure,
That it's according to my nature
And I can rally to its stature.

Thus spake Guru Gobind:
My Banda, you need never fear:
To dharma you'll be ever near.
You have the skill and the desire;
You will be blest with divine fire!
You are indeed a worthy seeker.
I will refresh you from the beaker
Of teachings from our guru line
So you may live the life divine.

By the beauty of your devotion
And the purity of your emotion,
Do burn away the crust of doubt
That from this secret's kept you out.
Now trusting me in full surrender
And pledging service to now render,
Breathe with ease; and calm your mind;
Make your heart toward Truth inclined.
Go within so that you can hear
These lessons with your inner ear.
For only then will your mind know
How doubts and conflicts easily go
Away by guru's intercession
Once you've entered the procession.
So cast away all selfish urge.
Of subtle doubts your mind now purge.

Thus said Banda:
O Guru! Thy words sweetly ring in my ears.
I would listen to thee for millions of years.
A profounder encounter I've not had before.
I open to thee to receive even more.
I surrender to thee from my innermost core
I am a mere supplicant now at thy door.

Thus spake Guru Gobind:
O most worthy disciple, you make my heart sing,
For I can to you my profound teaching bring,
Knowing you're able to imbibe its entirety,
And that your mission you'll finish with piety.
Because of everything you have learned,
O fearless Banda, you now have earned—
If, as you say, you really aspire—
The training to progress even higher.
You do acknowledge I can give it:
Now let me see if you can live it.

You were born, O chosen of God,
To tread the path that I have trod.
Allow me now to pre-inform you
Of my intent: I shall transform you!
And, to speak further of my mission,
To make you lead is my ambition.
You must merge your diverse learnings
And harness them to serve my yearnings
That you will lead my regimen
By your most noble acumen
And thereby set the dharma straight
At a brisk and efficient rate.
The time is now, and you're the man.
You have to do it: you only can.
For you are gentle and you are strong;
You can decipher right from wrong.
You are not swayed by selfish motive;
Your heart glows always like a votive.
This is your holy destiny:
To serve God in humanity.

Just as the stars spark in the night,
So will your deeds shine just as bright.
And when someone remembers me,
They'll think too of my Bairagi,
My chosen one, whose valor shone
With holy sweetness. He alone
Could put forth both—he put forth all.
As saint and leader did he enthrall.
In him, all opposites did mingle
And focus with an intent single.
Now decide, Banda. If you will it,
The calling's yours. Will you fulfill it?
I'm going to transform you now.
Are you prepared to take the vow?
Are you now ready to take up your mission

And see it to its resplendent fruition?
Its purpose is extremely broad in scope,
But for its success you give me great hope.

The mantle of destiny falls upon you
By virtue of disciplines you did pursue.
So now you are worthy to host the projection
Of people who see you as their soul's protection.
For their concept of God will 'pon you be transferred;
As you and the Lord in their hearts become blurred.
This is an awesome responsibility
Of astute ethical sensitivity.
Many have fallen beneath weight of this spell,
For its burden is awful, and few carry it well.
But you are a saint of unequaled humility—
Their admiration won't mar your tranquility.
Though self-proclaimed God-men lead others astray—
Keeping them ignorant and making them pay
To lose independence and the skill of free thinking,
Preying on weakness and devotion unblinking—
You are not selfish but truly concerned,
And know it is time that humanity learned
To live according to the great divine plan,
Rather than squabbling over custom and clan.
These selfish teachers wreak eons of trouble
Inviting derision and conflict to double.
They cater to those who can only pretend
To seek the Divine, and the dharma defend,
But who really just want to follow someone.
They don't want real teaching, and so they get none.
In India, the people seem especially liable
To under the sway of such men become pliable.
For they're trained from their youth to respect and not question
The teacher they choose, and to take his suggestion
On faith, without knowing its worth or its use,
And false teachers selfishly wage this abuse.

The poor unschooled seeker is victim to those
Unprincipled fakers who dharma oppose.
So let your wisdom shine forth, and let you accept
Any seeker who rallies, inept or adept.
Now gather them into the bosom of dharma;
Help them get freedom from bondage of karma!

Thus said Banda:
My Lord, I'm thy student, but thou lov'st me as though
I were a teacher in tune with Truth's flow.
Of thy noble lineage thou art the expression.
Yet I feel such skills are not in my possession.
I've been a soldier, and I've been a hermit;
If I'm a leader, I've yet to discern it.
And I am not really, in honesty, sure
What role such a leader should himself adjure.

Thus spake Guru Gobind:
Don't think of yourself as being unwise;
I know which destiny 'head of you lies.
Your past is done, and your future is sure:
Bairagi is reborn and is now Bahadur!
I have chosen you to serve as the instrument I need.
It's because of your nature that to this you accede.
You are perfectly suited to the task at hand,
With spiritual and worldly skill at your command.
You're a man of dharma; you're close to the Source.
Come up to your calling; use your inner force!
Inherit the wealth of your spiritual fathers,
Whose line you are in, and forget all the bothers
That impinge on your mind. You deserve
To receive, by their grace, the reserve
That has waited for you till this moment arrived.
By your own constant effort your spirit has thrived.
And has reached to the point where your gurus alone

Can lift you up to the celestial throne
That has sat empty among them until you were here
In the midst of that company you hold so dear.

16

The Guru Lineage

Thus said Banda:
I'm happy to hear there's a place for me there:
My heart sings in most grateful ecstasy rare.
I want to be there with the sacred sages
And be given the wisdom of all the ages.
But I don't understand how the wisdom is passed
So it remains pure from the first to the last.
Tell me, how is the lineage passed on through the ages?
And what are the ways to discern the true sages?

Thus spake Guru Gobind:
The guru lineage has a mysterious route.
It is passed on in ways most know little about.
The guru is drawn to the disciple who's ready—
Whose heart, mind, and soul are completely steady.
When the disciple attains to a lofty estate,
He presents himself at the innermost gate.
The gurus dwelling behind its keyless door
Attend to his callings as he does implore
The supreme Lord to admit him within.
And they, by his persistent love, determine
If he should enter. Then they open the portal
Whose threshold is seldom seen by any mortal.

Succession is passed on in only this way—
Bonds of birth or position don't hold any sway.
All succeeding gurus in our great tradition
Have attained to their status upon that condition—
That they're enlightened and have been anointed
By the line of the sages who them have appointed
To be caretakers on earth of the sacred teaching
That they cherish and want to maintain as far-reaching.
So the passage of power is thus carefully guarded
Lest any part of the heritage be somehow discarded
Or misused, distorted, diluted, or poorly fare
From lack of capacity on part of the heir.

The signs of a sage can be rightly perceived
When one-pointed mind remains undeceived
By projection or by unconscious desire
That keeps him ensnared in delusion's dark mire.
A sage, first of all, is without selfish motive:
The divine shines within as an eternal votive.
His posture's aligned and is perfectly still.
He can always help students by strength of his will.
Desires are vanquished; he is never perturbed;
His insight is pure and his mind undisturbed.
His awareness is constantly merged in the One:
Ego or barriers—of them he has none.
To him, all are equal shrines of the Divine,
And he dwells in infinite rapture sublime—
Yet he is active and serves all with love,
Reminding them of the Truth here and above.
His wisdom and knowledge of eternal law
Inspire others with devotion and awe.
But his major hallmark is the pure flow of love,
Which he bestows equally on all from above.

The role of the sage is upholder of dharma,
He helps burn the seeds of all impure karma.

He invisibly influences the chain of events
And many a man-made disaster prevents.
It is his nature to share divine light,
Reducing the pain of humanity's plight.
His presence on earth is a soothing, kind balm
That always gives peace and emotional calm.
He knows the potentials of those whom he guides,
And he shares with them secrets; from others he hides.
He gathers his students into his fold,
So that to them sacred words may be told.
And he plants in their hearts the seed of the Divine
That will blossom and reach to the top of the spine.
He guides all in his grace to the ultimate One,
And keeps coming back till the whole task is done.
He serves men in the world, yet he dwells in the void
And dispenses the nectar of love there enjoyed.
For humanity, roaming in the vale of despair,
There is no other solace that can even compare
With the sage's mere presence on this plane of existence.
Who can venture to count all his forms of assistance?

Thus said Banda:
Thy words are like nectar, and I thirst for more.
They refresh my spirit, its hope to restore.
Bestow on me now, my most revered Lord,
The gift of thy teaching—let it be poured
Over my being by grace of thy word.
Speak of the guru so my heart is stirred!

Thus spake Guru Gobind:
Without guru to teach us, we in darkness walk;
We lose our way, get distracted, or balk.
Without guru's help, self-conceit we can't burn;
Without his wise guidance, the Divine we can't earn.
He knows the true way, from inside guides our steps,
And bids us to tread the path our heart accepts.

Through faith in the guru the true Self is known;
By his words and actions the true path is shown.
Let his words, like seeds, grow, watered by love,
So they reach from your heart to the Truth above.

The guru's word is the breath of life;
The guru's word gives reprieve from strife.
The word of the guru is the sound within;
The word of the guru is the highest hymn.
The word of the guru is the music sublime,
The word of the guru pervades beyond time.
The guru's word a great secret resolves:
There is but one God, round which all revolves.
The guru's the Lords of the divine Trinity.
And he's the same as Mother Divinity.
Who follows the guru with heart, mind, and soul
Becomes one with the Lord and one with the Whole.

But remember, the guru is not a mere person;
Do not that mistake let your progress worsen.
He is not personality, not outward appearance,
But a wise inner force we give our adherence:
The guru resides within our very spirit,
But only those who listen in stillness can hear it.
So always stay inwardly tuned to his voice,
And give love to the world so all can rejoice.
Hail to the guru who dwells within all!
His transmuting spirit does good men enthrall.
'Pon the word of the guru can one safely cross
The great ocean of life, whose waves do him toss.
So constantly pray and remember his love;
Inspired you'll be from within and above.

17

The Divine Reality

Thus said Banda:
Thine exposition is superb and refined;
A difficult principle thou hast defined.
For more understanding I do ever yearn.
Please tell me the secrets I strive yet to learn.
What is the nature of the divine holy One,
And why of the Goddess hast thou sweetly sung?

Thus spake Guru Gobind:
To you do I tell the pure Truth sublime,
The nature of the great One Lord divine.
Nameless and homeless is He, with no caste,
Formless is He—boundless and vast.
He is the first Being, gracious, benign,
Unborn, ever perfect, eternal, divine.
B'yond distinction of nation, He has no desire.
With no outer likeness, to Him all aspire.
To the East or the West, look where you may,
All actions and beings are under His sway.
He pervades and prevails with compassion and love,
Permeating all, both below and above.
There is but one God, and Truth is His name.
Whatever He's called, He is always the same.

God, being Truth, is the one Light of all,
Who cares for all beings, from large to the small.
His expanse has no limit, no form has His face;
His abode is on earth and past realms of space.
Creation's His will, on which all life depends.
His being is now, was before, never ends.
He dwells in all times and in eternal Now:
In the world, yet transcendent—no one knows how.
All gifts in their proper way He bestows:
What they are, to whom—He alone knows.
Many have tried their best to describe Him;
All attributes and none they ascribe Him.

Where the breezes sing and blow,
Where the waters run and flow,
There is He beyond all strife,
Source and purveyor of life.
To Him no one can orders give.
As He wills, so do we live.
His holy seat is in all places;
His light reflects upon all faces.
Pure and changeless, He is ever true.
All difference levels beneath His view.
He made the flowers; His is the fire;
Nothing can happen without His desire.
He made variety; His are the seasons;
Whatever occurs, He knows the reasons.
His devotees are countless and of many kinds;
Their worship is varied by what's in their minds.
He is the focus of all of their praises;
They sing of His glory with myriad phrases.

Now I will tell you why I praise the Goddess.
To Her have I given my soul's solemn promise
To serve Her as loving and loyal devotee.
For none is more revered than She is by me.

The strength of the Mother is my great shield;
By Her is dharma's fate ever sealed.
She is the source of adamant strength
That upholds the dharma for whatever length.
To Her do all turn as a final resort
When no other power can adharma thwart.
She is tender and loving with Her delicate child—
But if it is threatened, She rampages wild.
Then no force of man can Her fierce wrath assuage
As She slays aggressors in motherly rage.
With blood-dripping fangs and flesh-ripping claws,
She prevails o'er all foes to enforce dharma's laws.
When all of Her weapons and ire She assembles,
The whole of creation marvels and trembles.
Dreadful Her visage and awesome Her dance;
She vanquishes evil with Her fiery glance.
Frightful the incomparable power She wields!
Inevitable that to Her the enemy yields!
She is Mother Durga, alive as the sword
That's carried aloft by dharma's warlord.
She is the power that in his veins flows;
Hers is the might that makes fierce his blows.

Long have my people loved and adored Her;
For freedom and victory have they oft implored Her.
Sites to Her homage in our land abound.
Anandpur itself is on Her sacred ground.
Even Vishnu and Brahma and Sri Maheswara
Bow to Her power as upholder of dharma.
The gods on their knees admit Her awesome dignity
And beg Her return to Her former benignity.
Soaked is my soul with the fervor of Shakti—
She showers Her grace in battle and bhakti.
She's the inspiration of poet and warrior;
She is the source of builder and destroyer.
When moral order is threatened by evil ravages,

She is the sword that dispatches the savages.
Thus every Sikh should carry the sword,
remembering always the Name of the Lord.

Thus said Banda:
Thine endless devotion to the Mother Divine
Has filled me with sacred wonder sublime.
I take Her up as my sword and my shield.
Her unconquerable fire will I ever wield!
She bathes my spirit in rapturous zeal
That no austere practice e'er brought me to feel.
O Guru, thy speech does so marvel my mind
That comparison to it I could never find.
By listening to thy most rapturous word,
The divine in my heart has been ever stirred.
Do tell me the way to retain this high feeling—
My heart, mind, and soul are in Divine reeling.

Thus spake Guru Gobind:
The way to retain it is simple indeed:
To repeat God's Name is all that you need.
Throughout your life's ambrosial hours
Preserve the Name as sacred flowers.
Think on the Name always in your heart.
Uplift yourself; accept your part—
The Name will reveal what you need to know;
Its effects on your face and behavior will show.
By repeating the Name, one attains the Divine,
And does his whole person completely refine.
Belief in the Name helps one to avoid
Mistakes by which he could be destroyed.
If the mind is scattered and it's polluted,
God's Holy Name should then be saluted,
For through singular focus on it alone
Are calmness and purity of mind ever known.
Those who remember the Holy Name

And strive for it purely, victory claim.
Repeat the Lord's Name—while you serve—
Then you'll enjoy spiritual verve.
Repeat within ever the Name of the Lord;
Keep your heart tuned to that divine chord.
Let this refrain, "Thou alone art,"
Be the song that resounds deep in your heart.
Let your inner life always proclaim
The splendor and love of the Holy Name!

18

Self-Surrender

Thus said Banda:
I fall at thy feet in eternal surrender!
My heart is in bliss to perceive thy vast splendor!
Accept, please, my life in service complete.
I place all I am at thy sacred feet.

Thus spake Guru Gobind:
Arise, O my Banda! Your dharma now calls.
Embrace Providence, lest your fortress falls.

Thus said Banda:
I will cling to thy feet in full supplication.
I give thee my life in full dedication.
I have taken rebirth as thy spiritual son.
By thy grace the evil will soon be undone.
Let me with sword flash and strike against evil,
Cutting its root out in the sacred upheaval.
May I, O Guru, completely surrender
And merge in the Infinite's wondrous splendor.
May I be anointed by thee here and now
So I will have grace to accomplish my vow.

Thus spake Guru Gobind:
O Banda, you have reached that high state

Where disciple and guru culminate
Their work and join together as one
To continue their mission until it is done.
Mine is the path of fierce warring steel;
All I can offer you is an ordeal.
There is no assurance that victory you'll win
Nor that new eras of peace will begin.
But one thing is definite—it is sure—
You will as a martyr die happy and pure.
As the leader of our mission, you will acquaint
The world with the nature of a true warrior-saint.
I accept you; you surrender to me—
No greater alliance can there ever be.

Thus said Banda:
I am fulfilled to be by thee so blessed.
Life for thy cause would be the highest
Honor toward which a man could ever aspire.
Following you I renounce all desire.
The only need that I have now
Is ample time to live my vow.

Thus spake Guru Gobind:
Time is a factor we cannot ignore,
For neither of us has very much more.
You must immerse yourself in relentless action,
And I must prepare for my final transaction.
My quest to find you has ended well:
I am with the Infinite free to dwell.
You have come as was destined, so now I am through;
The people and dharma rely now on you.
If those who wronged me I strongly subdue,
My motive for acting some might misconstrue
As a vendetta, or desire to reign,
Instead of the balance of dharma regain.
I'm but an instrument of the Divine;

The battles I wage are His, never mine.
Lest others have reason to unjustly accuse
Selfish motive of us, it's you I do choose
To continue the mission in which we believe.
I give you the duties, and now you receive.
The Lord designated me to assign
The one who will work for Him when I resign.
For the Divine's will is that my garment be shed
In one month, and that my men should be led
By my belov'd Banda, whose bravery soars.
I have played my role. Now you will play yours!
Lead my men into battle: they're thirsting for action.
Be true to dharma; give the soul satisfaction.
My soldiers will offer their lives for dharma
And thus will uphold their collective karma.
Long have they been from their family and home;
Long are the days when on horseback they roam.
You are most blessed to be worthy to lead them.
To victory 'gainst evil, do rapidly speed them!

Thus said Banda:
Humbly I embrace thy exalted mission.
Before I begin, may I have benediction?
Anoint me into thy pantha, I implore,
So I may be one with the Khalsa I adore.

Thus spake Guru Gobind:
Ordained by my word are you already in spirit,
I now proclaim it for others to hear it.
I give you five symbols to wear as a sign:
As you live and die you are the best of mine.
I give you the nectar of immortality,
So you expand to universality.
Now and forever you are a Singh!
Now to humanity the dharma bring!
No longer will Bairagi Madho Das endure:

Arise to your men, Banda Singh Bahadur!
All my sons to the holy dharma I did give.
O best of my sons—fight as such while you live,
And die in the same bliss-filled worthiest way,
So you may enjoy the same rapture as they.
And now my own arrows to you I bequeath:
Use them with skill before this plane you leave.

Thus said Banda:
Thou art my real father, whose lineage and name
From now to eternity I do proclaim.
I am thy lion and thy loyal son.
Thou and I are now eternally one.
By the holy nectar I sipped from thy hands,
In me divine consciousness ever expands.

Thus spake Guru Gobind:
Blessed are you, my holy son!
You are my qualified and chosen one.
Now we must act, for time is so short.
To my eager army you must now report.
In spirit be you all ever glorious!
In battle be you always victorious!
And may you e'er dwell within pure, divine rapture.
For dharma the hearts of the people now capture.
Lead them to live by their guru tradition,
Bringing the essence of love to fruition.
The true Sikh's a selfless and faithful server
Who repeats God's Name with one-pointed fervor.
Sikhs chant the hymns with perfect devotion
And uphold the dharma with purest emotion.
True Sikhs all live by the Sri Adi Grantha
And always remember the one sacred mantra:
"*Aum* is the form and one Holy Name true
Of the awesome, amazing, and supreme Guru."
They repeat these words in their hearts to imbue:
"*Ek omkar satanam sri wahe guru!*"

Glossary

adharma. Unrighteousness. Unwholesome practices that disturb individual and social harmony and thereby prevent the growth of humanity.

Adi Granth. The sacred scripture of Sikhism. The compilation of the teachings of Guru Nanak Dev and many other sages of the tradition. After the guru lineage stopped with Guru Gobind Singh, the tenth guru, this scripture itself substituted for a living guru. It is the same as the Sri Guru Granth Sahib.

ahimsa. Non-injury, non-hurting, and non-killing; one of the five yamas or behavioral restraints, also known as the "great dharma": the highest of all observances leading to the spiritual goal.

amrit. Ambrosia, nectar. It is used in initiating a Sikh into the Khalsa and conveys the idea of attaining immortality and eternal bliss.

Aryan. Literally, the "noble one." The people of India who explored the wisdom of the Vedas and the Upanishads and contributed to the growth of Indian culture and civilization.

avatar. A divine incarnation. After accomplishing the purpose of life, realized beings can choose to incarnate onto the physical plane in order to serve humanity.

bairagi. One who has mastered vairagya—dispassion, non-attachment.

Bhagavad Gita. "Song of God." A famous scripture of philosophy and spirituality written in the form of a dialogue between an enlightened master, Krishna, and his prepared student, Arjuna. This scripture is an excerpt from the voluminous Sanskrit epic, The Mahabharata.

bhakta. An adherent of the path of love and devotion.

bhakti. Devotion. Bhakti yoga is the spiritual path that expounds the methods of channelling and transforming human emotions into divine ecstasy. Selfless love and service are the central practices of this path.

Bharata. An ancient name of India. Its use was resumed after independence in 1947.

brahmin. Literally "the knower of the Vedas." Ideally a brahmin is he who commits himself or herself solely to study and teaching, receiving and giving. While practicing personally, he or she motivates others to follow the path of Truth.

Buddhism. The system of philosophy and practice expounded by Buddha, who taught during the fifth century, B.C.

Dassam Granth. Guru Gobind Singh's compositions, some of which are prayed daily by Sikhs today.

dharma. The eternal law that holds and maintains the individual as well as social life. It also refers to one's duty or destiny in life.

guru. The spiritual master endowed with the capacity of dispelling the darkness of ignorance and leading seekers on the path of light.

gurudwaras. Literally, "the gateway to gurudeva." The temples where followers of Sikhism conduct their worship and services.

Hindu. The term originally referred to the place or country named after the river Sindhu. Later it denoted the citizens of India who, in those days, believed in the philosophy and practices taught by the Vedic sages. Upon the rise of Islam and Christianity in India, this term was used to designate those who were not associated with Islam and Christianity.

Islam. A monotheistic religion with Muhammed as its first prophet. The main scripture of this religion is the Koran. It is the principal religion of the Arabian states as well as Iran, Turkey, Afghanistan, Pakistan, and other West Asian countries.

Jainism. A religion based on twenty-four saints, beginning with Rishabbhadeva and ending with Mahavira. Around the sixth century B.C., Mahavira founded Jainism as a distinct school of philosophy and spirituality. It still flourishes in various parts of India.

Japji. A highly profound but short book of prayers by Guru Nanak Dev. Ideally, it is to be recited daily by sincere Sikhs.

karma. Action. It includes the law of action and reaping the results of action.

Khalsa. The organization of Sikhs that has a sense of brotherhood among all and is committed to the guru's mission and the defense of dharma. The Khalsa order was established in 1699 by Guru Gobind Singh.

Koranic. The rules and laws as described in the Koran, the sacred scripture of Islam.

kshatriya. Literally, "he who protects the oppressed." At the end of the Vedic period, this term was used to denote the group of people who were committed to the protection of the nation, society, and humanitarian values.

maya. Illusion. The power to veil and distort Reality on an individual and universal level.

Mogul. Refers to the Turks and Afghans of the Muslim faith who overran northern India in the thirteenth century and remained in power for almost 600 years.

Monism. A non-dualistic philosophy formally founded by Shankaracharya in the eighth century A.D.

Muslim. A follower of Islam who surrenders his thought, speech, and action to the will of God, Allah.

Nath sadhu. A saint from the Natha order, which was founded by Gorakha or Matsyendra.

Nawab. The name for a regional governor during the Mogul rule of India.

pandit. A learned man well-versed in the scriptures who follows the path of spirituality.

Panj Piare. "Five devoted spirits beloved of the Guru"; the five disciples of Guru Gobind Singh who answered his request for the sacrifice of their lives as a sign of their devotion.

pantha. The spiritual path.

pranams. A gesture of respect and deep devotion given to a sage or guru.

prasad. An offering of food to a deity; also such an offering received from a sage or guru that carries his or her blessings.

raja. King. The feudal lords who governed territories in India.

Ravana. The villain of the Ramayana, the epic tale that describes the life of Rama, a divine king of India.

rishi. A seer. An enlightened sage fully attuned with the wisdom of Truth.

sadhus. Those who are committed to sadhana, spiritual practice.

samadhi. Spiritual absorption: the eighth rung of raja yoga. The tranquil state of mind in which fluctuations of the mind no longer arise.

sannyas. Renunciation. The spiritual path in which a student learns how to transcend worldly temptations and fearlessly renounce the world to attain the supreme Goal.

Shakti. The divine force, the prime cause of the universe.

siddha. An accomplished master who, through sincere practice and grace, has acquired higher powers.

siddhis. Spiritual powers that transcend normal human limitations.

Sri Guru Granth Sahib. The scripture compiled by the fifth guru, Arjan Dev, and recompiled by the tenth guru, Guru Gobind Singh. It contains hymns of six of the Sikh gurus and many other saints. It is the same as the Adi Granth.

Sufi. One who strives to attain a state of union with Supreme beauty and joy. Sufism is derived from Vedanta and the mystical aspect of Islam.

tapas. Literally fire or heat; the third moral observance of yoga. It includes austerities to purify the mind and senses.

Upanishads. The final portion of the Vedas; the ancient scriptures containing the wisdom of the sages. The philosophy of Vedanta is based on the Upanishads.

Vaishnava. A sub-branch of Hinduism that emphasizes the worship of Vishnu, the preserver of the universe.

Vedanta. The system of Indian philosophy that expounds the theory of the Upanishads.

Vedas. The sourcebook of knowledge; the revealed wisdom experienced by the great sages in deep meditation.

yoga. The school of Indian philosophy that was systematized by the sage Patanjali, codifier of the Yoga Sutras. Generally it means "yoke," referring to the uniting of the individual self and the universal Self.

yogi. One who follows the path of discipline to attain a state of balance among all aspects of his personality: body, breath, mind, and soul.

About the Author

Yogi, scientist, philosopher, humanitarian, and mystic poet, Swami Rama is the founder and spiritual head of the Himalayan International Institute of Yoga Science and Philosophy, with its headquarters in Honesdale, Pennsylvania and therapy and educational centers throughout the world. He was born in a Himalayan valley of Uttar Pradesh, India, in 1925 and was initiated and anointed in early childhood by a great sage of the Himalayas. He studied with many adepts, and then traveled to Tibet to study with his grandmaster. From 1949 to 1952 he held the prestige and dignity of Shankaracharya (spiritual leader) in Karvirpitham in the South of India. He then returned to the Himalayas to intensify his meditative practices in the cave monasteries and to establish an ashram in Rishikesh.

Later he continued his investigation of Western psychology and philosophy at several European universities, and he taught in Japan before coming to the United States in 1969. The following year he served as a consultant to the Voluntary Controls Project of the Research Department of the Menninger Foundation. There he demonstrated, under laboratory conditions, precise control over his autonomic nervous system and brain. The findings of that research increased the scientific community's understanding of the human ability to control autonomic functioning and to attain previously unrecognized levels of consciousness.

Shortly thereafter, Swami Rama founded the Himalayan Institute as a means to synthesize the ancient teachings of the East with the modern approaches of the West. He has played a major role in bringing the insights of yoga psychology and philosophy to the attention of the physicians and psychologists of the West. He continues to teach students around the world while intensifying his writing and meditative practices. He is the author of many books and currently spends most of his time in the mountains of Northern India and in Pennsylvania, U.S.A.

The main building of the national headquarters, Honesdale, Pa.

The Himalayan Institute

The Himalayan International Institute of Yoga Science and Philosophy of the U.S.A. is a nonprofit organization devoted to the scientific and spiritual progress of modern humanity. Founded in 1971 by Sri Swami Rama, the Institute combines Western and Eastern teachings and techniques to develop educational, therapeutic, and research programs for serving people in today's world. The goals of the Institute are to teach meditational techniques for the growth of individuals and their society, to make known the harmonious view of world religions and philosophies, and to undertake scientific research for the benefit of humankind.

This challenging task is met by people of all ages, all walks of life, and all faiths who attend and participate in the Institute courses and seminars. These programs, which are given on a continuing basis, are designed in order that one may discover for oneself how to live more creatively. In the words of Swami Rama, "By being aware of one's own potential and abilities, one can become a perfect citizen, help the nation, and serve humanity."

The Institute has branch centers and affiliates throughout the United States. The 422-acre campus of the national headquarters, located in the Pocono Mountains of northeastern Pennsylvania, serves as the coordination center for all the Institute activities, which include a wide variety of innovative programs in education, research, and therapy, combining Eastern and Western approaches to self-awareness and self-directed change.

SEMINARS, LECTURES, WORKSHOPS, and CLASSES are available throughout the year, providing intensive training and experience in such topics as Superconscious

Meditation, hatha yoga, philosophy, psychology, and various aspects of personal growth and holistic health. The *Himalayan News*, a free bimonthly publication, announces the current programs.

The RESIDENTIAL and SELF-TRANSFORMATION PROGRAMS provide training in the basic yoga disciplines—diet, ethical behavior, hatha yoga, and meditation. Students are also given guidance in a philosophy of living in a community environment.

The PROGRAM IN EASTERN STUDIES AND COMPARATIVE PSYCHOLOGY offers a unique and systematic synthesis of Western empirical sources and Eastern introspective science. Masters and Doctoral-level studies may be pursued through cross-registration with several accredited colleges and universities.

The five-day STRESS MANAGEMENT/PHYSICAL FITNESS PROGRAM offers practical and individualized training that can be used to control the stress response. This includes biofeedback, relaxation skills, exercise, diet, breathing techniques, and meditation.

A yearly INTERNATIONAL CONGRESS, sponsored by the Institute, is devoted to the scientific and spiritual progress of modern humanity. Through lectures, workshops, seminars, and practical demonstrations, it provides a forum for professionals and lay people to share their knowledge and research.

The ELEANOR N. DANA RESEARCH LABORATORY is the psychophysiological laboratory of the Institute, specializing in research on breathing, meditation, holistic therapies, and stress and relaxed states. The laboratory is fully equipped for exercise stress testing and psychophysiological measurements, including brain waves, patterns of respiration, heart rate changes, and muscle tension. The staff investigates Eastern teachings through studies based on Western experimental techniques.

Himalayan Institute Publications

Living with the Himalayan Masters	Swami Rama
Lectures on Yoga	Swami Rama
A Practical Guide to Holistic Health	Swami Rama
Choosing a Path	Swami Rama
Inspired Thoughts of Swami Rama	Swami Rama
Freedom from the Bondage of Karma	Swami Rama
Book of Wisdom (Ishopanishad)	Swami Rama
Enlightenment Without God	Swami Rama
Exercise Without Movement	Swami Rama
Life Here and Hereafter	Swami Rama
Marriage, Parenthood, and Enlightenment	Swami Rama
Path of Fire and Light	Swami Rama
Perennial Psychology of the Bhagavad Gita	Swami Rama
Love Whispers	Swami Rama
Celestial Song/Gobind Geet	Swami Rama
Creative Use of Emotion	Swami Rama, Swami Ajaya
Science of Breath	Swami Rama, Rudolph Ballentine, M.D., Alan Hymes, M.D.
Yoga and Psychotherapy	Swami Rama, Rudolph Ballentine, M.D., Swami Ajaya
Yoga-sutras of Patanjali	Usharbudh Arya, D.Litt.
Superconscious Meditation	Usharbudh Arya, D.Litt.
Mantra and Meditation	Usharbudh Arya, D.Litt.
Philosophy of Hatha Yoga	Usharbudh Arya, D.Litt.
Meditation and the Art of Dying	Usharbudh Arya, D.Litt.
God	Usharbudh Arya, D.Litt.
Psychotherapy East and West: A Unifying Paradigm	Swami Ajaya, Ph.D.
Yoga Psychology	Swami Ajaya, Ph.D.
Psychology East and West	Swami Ajaya, Ph.D. (ed.)
Meditational Therapy	Swami Ajaya, Ph.D. (ed.)
Diet and Nutrition	Rudolph Ballentine, M.D.
Joints and Glands Exercises	Rudolph Ballentine, M.D. (ed.)
Theory and Practice of Meditation	Rudolph Ballentine, M.D. (ed.)
Freedom from Stress	Phil Nuernberger, Ph.D.
Science Studies Yoga	James Funderburk, Ph.D.
Homeopathic Remedies	Drs. Anderson, Buegel, Chernin
Hatha Yoga Manual I	Samskrti and Veda
Hatha Yoga Manual II	Samskrti and Judith Franks

Seven Systems of Indian Philosophy	R. Tigunait, Ph.D.
Swami Rama of the Himalayas	L. K. Misra, Ph.D. (ed.)
Philosophy of Death and Dying	M. V. Kamath
Practical Vedanta of Swami Rama Tirtha	Brandt Dayton (ed.)
The Swami and Sam	Brandt Dayton
Yoga Psychology and the Beatitudes	S. Arpita, Ph.D.
Yoga and Christianity	Justin O'Brien, D.Th.
Himalayan Mountain Cookery	Martha Ballentine
The Yoga Way Cookbook	Himalayan Institute
Meditation in Christianity	Himalayan Institute
Art and Science of Meditation	Himalayan Institute
Therapeutic Value of Yoga	Himalayan Institute
Chants from Eternity	Himalayan Institute
Spiritual Diary	Himalayan Institute
Blank Books	Himalayan Institute

Write for a free mail order catalog describing all our publications.